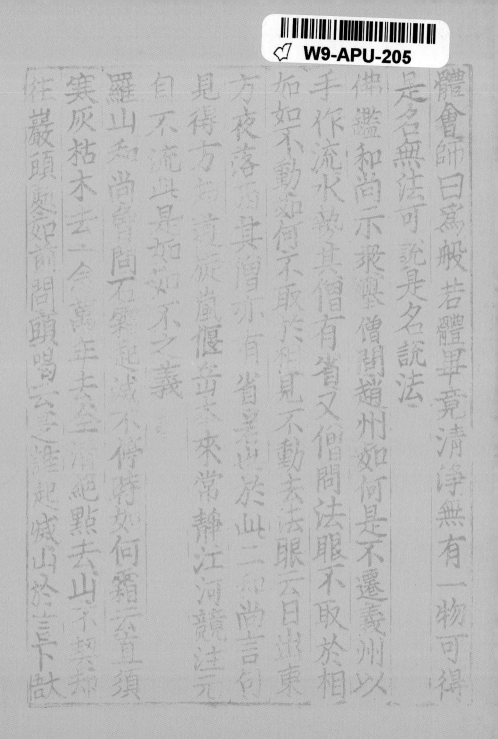

體會師曰為般若體畢竟清淨無有一物可得

是名無法可說是名說法

佛鑑和尚示眾墨僧問趙州如何是不遷義州以

手作流水狀其僧有省又僧問法眼不取於相

如如不動如何得不取於相見不動末法眼云日出東

方夜落西其僧亦有省是近於此二師尚言句

見得方諦道灰嵐優曇朵來常靜江河競注元

自不流此是如如不之義

羅山和尚曾問石霜起滅不停時如何霜云直須

寒灰枯木云一念萬年去絕點去山不契却

往巖頭憂如前問頭喝云是誰起滅山於言下歇

是十分真用意勇猛丈夫却須恁麼切莫

不須念二聖改名為指南矣

雖然辜負閻羅老子一場懡㦬來得恁麼要講坐禪不

動坐禪猶如章偈志爭

而今即從來縱頭腦物皆

白云從來縱髮一不曾發若閑坐禪成底

東京落西

大珠禪師因僧問一切眾生有佛性也何師云作

佛用是佛性你戲用具性作眾生用是眾生性

性無形相隨用立多名經云一切賢聖皆以無為法

而有差別又僧問無法可說是名說法禪師如何

Jikji, light from the East Ⅱ

Jikji,
light from the East
II

Cheongju Early Printing Museum

Preface

After printing technology was first invented, engraved woodblocks or wooden movable types were most widely used to print books. Though they were time consuming methods, time was not a big issue because demand for books was not huge back then. However, the increase of writings themselves as well as demand for them led to attempts to change the existing printing methods, which resulted in the development of movable metal type, a new way of printing. The emergence of the metal movable type printing brought a remarkable change in printing method while reinvigorating the existing woodblock printing, which remained as the mainstream method until the end of the Joseon dynasty. Although it is not known exactly when the movable metal type printing started, it seemed that it was not something very special for Goryeo, a small state in the East, to cast movable metal type sets and print books with them.

The book, "*Jikji* II, the Light from the East" introduces the printing culture of Goryeo, which invented movable metal type, while comparing its impact on societies in two different cultures and environment of Goryeo and Europe. I sincerely hope this book would provide you with an opportunity to move away from the West-oriented view that the technology of Europe was superior and appreciate that the movable metal type printing was the best choice and invention that reflected respective culture of two different societies.

December 2018
Director of Cheongju Early Printing Museum Oh, Youngtack

Table of Contents

The Culture of Movable Metal Type Printing in Goryeo

The *Jikji* and the 42-line Bible

"Jikji," UNESCO's Memory of the World Programme and Cheongju

The Culture of Movable Metal Type Printing in Goryeo

Woo Jin-woong

Full-time Researcher, Data Division, The Korean Study Institute

I

Introduction

Korea has taken an important position in the world history of printing. There are a number of examples that prove Korea's outstanding printing culture in the annals of global printing history: Baegun hwasang chorok buljo *jikji*simcheyojeol (白雲和尙抄錄佛祖直指心體要節, the second volume of "Anthology of Great Buddhist Priests' Zen Teachings," to be referred as *Jikji* hereafter), the world's oldest extant book printed with movable metal type at Heungdeoksa Temple in Cheongju in 1377; Mugujeonggwang Daedaranigyeong (無垢淨光大陀羅尼經, a sutra (Buddhist canonical scripture)), the oldest book printed with woodblocks in 751; and Goryeo Daejanggyeong (the Tripiṭaka Koreana—a Korean collection of the Tripiṭaka (Buddhist scriptures and the Sanskrit word for "three baskets"), the best of Korean Tripitaka . In particular, historical records and facts tell us that Korea developed movable metal type printing for the first time in the world, which was 78 years before the development of Gutenberg's movable type, which has been selected as the best human invention for the past 1000 years.

Printing technology can be developed only when sociocultural and technical factors, such as the dissemination of letters, the demand for books, and advanced printing technique, are met. From early days of its history, highly sophisticated Buddhist culture were developed in Korea and Koreans were involved in religious activities. From the Silla period, people had a high zeal for education, indicating a growing demand for literature. At the same time, it had satisfied many of the technical conditions required for the development of printing technology. The printing culture, at the beginning of the Three Kingdoms of Korea, was started with stamps, stone monuments, wooden tablets, and manuscripts of Buddhist scriptures, and by the time of Silla, woodblock printing had started and was gradually penetrating society. Silla's woodblock printing was passed down to Goryeo and reached its peak as the demand for literature, mostly for Buddhist scriptures, grew rapidly thanks to the policy to revere Buddhism at the national level. As a result, two large-scale Tripitaka publication projects were conducted. The Goryeo period started to

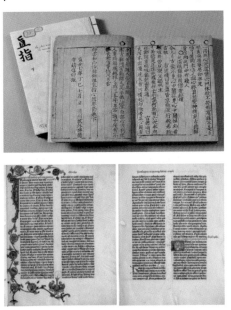

"Jikji" and the Gutenberg Bible

use movable metal type pieces to print literature, including *Jikji*, at Heungdeoksa Temple in Cheongju. As movable metal type was passed down to Joseon, the technology was advanced further, and by the time of the later Joseon dynasty, it became possible to cast various kinds of movable metal type pieces depending on their purpose and practical use, which was unprecedented in the world's printing history. This had an enormous impact on the distribution of books and the dissemination and sharing of knowledge.

Under the title "The Culture of Movable Metal Type Printing in Goryeo," this article provides an overview of woodblock printing before and after the Goryeo dynasty and the extant woodblock printed books while elaborating on the technical and social cultural backgrounds for the development of movable metal type during the Goryeo period, and the influence of Goryeo's movable type printing on Joseon.

II

Goryeo Dynasty at the Full Blossoming of Printing Culture

1. The Golden Age of Woodblock Printing

The development of printing technology was closely related to religion. Buddhism was first introduced to Korea in 372 when King Sosurim of Goguryeo ascended to the throne. After that, Buddhism had a profound impact on everything from the politics to society, culture, and art as it became the state religion of Unified Silla and Goryeo. In particular, during the Goryeo dynasty, it had become a religious belief that guarantees the well-being of the state and individuals. Out of the belief that the state could overcome difficulties, defeat foreign invasions, and defend the state with the power of Buddha, temples were constructed across the nation and Buddhist scriptures were actively published, bringing about the development of printing. In addition, the Silla dynasty had also satisfied most of the conditions required for a printing culture to be created. Before Goryeo, Silla could make paper, and produced and exported high quality ink sticks to China. It had also possessed the sculpture techniques to carve letters and drawings and the technique to engrave a Buddha and a pagoda on woodblocks to print in large quantities. The combination of these conditions for printing with book production technique laid the foundation for woodblock printing technology. Although scholars in Asia and Europe have different opinions on the time when woodblock printing first occurred, the most convincing opinion is between the late 7th century and the early 8th century. The extant early woodblock prints are important evidence to support such an opinion.

Mugujeonggwang Daedaranigyeong, printed with woodblocks during Silla, is known to be the world's oldest woodblock print. The Buddhist scripture, which was placed in Seokgatap (a stone pagoda) while rebuilding the existing Bulguksa Temple in 751 (the 10th year of King Gyeongdeok), was printed 20 years before Japan's Hyakumanto Darani (The one million pagodas and Dharani prayers). Korea's Dharani scripture shows very sophisticated engraving techniques and is in better shape than the Japanese one.

Goryeo, which inherited the woodblock printing technique from Silla, achieved a remarkable technical advancement as woodblock printing became widely used by the central government and temples. Goryeo promoted Buddhism as a state religion and published all kinds of Buddhist literature.

During the Goryeo dynasty, the educational system was expanded and related systems were changed to give preferential treatment to scholars, and as a result, eminent scholars became high-ranking officials. The state examination was administered to recruit talent and the role of Hyangyo (local Confucian schools) was expanded to a large extent. Against this social background, by the later part of the Goryeo dynasty, the central and provincial government offices, temples, and individuals published literature on a variety of themes from Buddhist literature, Confucian books, history books, and anthologies, and the number of literature publications increased rapidly. It was Goryeo that wrote a new chapter in the history of printing culture with its invention of movable metal type, along with the existing manuscripts and woodblock prints.

In the early years of Goryeo, it inherited the woodblock printing technique from Silla. After that, numerous books from the period of the Five Dynasties and Ten Kingdoms (907-960) and the early period of the North Sung dynasty (960-1127) were imported from China, and with the publication of Daejanggyeong, woodblock printing flourished in the 11th century. During the Joseon period, which inherited its printing culture from Goryeo, publishers became diversified over a long period of time and various techniques were used to publish various literature in large volumes. Published literature was widely distributed among the intellectual class and those with power, as well as ordinary people, which provided an opportunity to share and spread knowledge and information.

If Silla was the period when the printing culture started to bud in Korea, it was Goryeo when the printing culture blossomed. At the same time, it was Goryeo that laid the foundation for modern-day Korea to be inundated with information as it went through the period of Joseon into modern times. The next part will focus on the extant woodblock prints of Goryeo.

1.1 Bohyeopindaranigyeong

Bohyeopindaranigyeong (寶篋印陀羅尼經, a sutra—Buddhist canonical scripture) is the oldest woodblock print of Goryeo, which was printed at Chongjisa Temple in 1007 (the 10th year of King Mokjong). The original title was "Ilcheyeorae simbimil jeonsinsari bohyeopindaranigyeong" (一切如來心秘密全身舍利寶篋印陀羅尼經). Its printing state was superior to Mugujeonggwang Daedaranigyeong, which proved the technical advancement after publication of the latter, and it was the first woodblock print that had publication information. It is Korea's oldest extant woodblock print book and highly sophisticated illustrations were included. The small-sized scroll printed with woodblocks had pub-

Bohyeopin daranigyeong(1007)

lication information followed by illustrations of Buddhist scriptures, and the main texts had an average of nine characters in each line.

The imprint, "高麗國摠持寺主眞念 廣濟大師釋弘哲敬造 寶篋印經板印施普安 佛塔中供養時 統和二十五年丁未歲記" gives information about the publishing temple, publisher, the title of the book, and the year of publication. This illustration shows the content of the Buddhist scriptures, which is about seeking enlightenment from agonies and obtaining well-being after defeating all kinds of disasters and fear.

1.2 Goryeo Daejanggyeong

Daejanggyeong (Tripitaka) could be considered the most representative woodblock print of Goryeo. Gaebo Daejanggyeong, which was engraved by the command of the first King of the Sung Dynasty of China during the era named Gaebo (968-976), was imported by Han Eon-gong in 991 (the 10th year of King Seongjong of Goryeo). It had a huge impact on the production of Goryeo Daejanggyeong. The production of *Chojodaejanggyeong* (初雕大藏經, The First Tripitaka Koreana, the first engraved complete canon of Buddhist scriptures in the Goryeo Dynasty) was meaningful by itself, but held a greater meaning in that it laid the foundation for the production of *Jaejodaejanggyeong* (再雕大藏經, also called Palman Daejanggyeong, a complete Buddhist cannon, made after Chojodaejanggyeong was destroyed during Mongolia's invasion in 1232) 200 years later.

The publication of Daejanggyeong started in an effort to overcome difficulties facing Goryeo, due to frequent invasions by the Kitan, using the power of Buddha by engraving Buddhist scriptures on woodblocks. Behind such religious perspectives, however, it was intended to show the status of Goryeo as a state with a vibrant culture through frequent exchanges with the Sung dynasty of China.

Daebanggwang Bul hwaeomgyeong (Chojodaejanggyeong)

Currently, about 250 pieces of Chojodaejanggyeong are left in Korea and some 2,500 pieces are at Nanzenji Temple in Kyoto and in Tsushima, Japan. The basis for Chojodaejanggyeong was *Gaebo Daejanggyeong,* the Buddhist Scripture of China's Sung dynasty, and some contents from Daejanggyeong of the Kitan were also included to some extent. The engraving period was from 1011 (the 2nd year of King Hyeonjong) to 1087 (the 4th year of King Seonjong), and additional engraving was made as needed.

Jaejodaejanggyeong stored in Haeinsa Temple

Jaejodaejanggyeong, another Daejanggyeong of Goryeo, was engraved for sixteen years from 1236 (the 23rd year of King Gojong) to 1251 (the 38th year of King Gojong) at Daejangdogam (大藏都監, the headquarters of a government administration temporarily established for the publication) in *Ganghwado* and it branch offices. After the engraving of *Chojodaejanggyeong* was completed, engraved woodblocks were stored in Heungwangsa Temple in Gaeseong and moved to Buinsa Temple on Palgongsan Mountain in Daegu. After they were burnt during Mongolia's invasion in 1232, Goryeo decided to engrave another set to overcome the national crisis using the power of Buddha, and engraving offices named Daejangdogam were established for the large-scale national project. *Jaejodaejanggyeong* is also known as *Palman Daejanggyeong* because of the number of woodblocks with scriptures engraved on them. Completed Buddhist scripture woodblocks were first stored in the Daejanggyeong repository in *Ganghwado*, and moved to Haeinsa Temple in Hapcheon, Gyeongnam in 1398 (the 9th year of King Taejo) and have been there ever since.

Jaejodaejanggyeong is the oldest among all the Daejanggyeongs in the world and has been globally recognized for the excellence of its printing technique. In 2007, the woodblocks of Goryeo Daejanggyeong were inscribed on the UESCNO Memory of the World Register, letting the world know the excellence and value of Korea's woodblock printing culture during the Goryeo dynasty.

1.3 Gyojang

Gyojang (敎藏) was a set of annotated books, written by Buddhist monks with academic knowledge on Daejanggyeong after Chojodaejanggyeong was completed. The Buddhist monk Uicheon (1055-1101), the National Preceptor compiled "Gyojang Chongnok" in three volumes which contained a list of the 1,010 copies and 4,857 books he collected, including 400 written studies by Silla monks, as well as studies and commentaries on Daejanggyeong from the Sung Dynasty of China, the Kitan, and Japan. Gyojangdogam was established in Heungwangsa Temple to publish Gyojang based on the list. The engraving of Gyojang was started in the spring of 1091 after the compilation of Gyojang Chongnok was completed in 1102 (the 7th year of Sukjong), a year after he passed away. Since Gyojang has 20 to 22 characters for each line, its most distinctive feature is that its relatively small characters are densely engraved.

There are other woodblock-printed materials of Goryeo: "*Geumganggyeong*" (the Diamond Sutra), "*Seonmun samga yeomsongjip*" (Book of Reciting for Zen Buddhism)—which were published by individuals such as Choe, Chung-heon and different families including Choe U, and other Buddhist scriptures, and "*Jungyong juja hongmun*" (Questions and Answers on the Doctrine of the Mean), "*Geunsarok*" (Reflections on Things at Hand)—books imported from the Yuan Dynasty of China and reprinted and published in Jinju and other provincial offices. There are also the anthologies: "*Geubam seonsaeng sijip*," an anthology of Min, Sapyeong (1295-1359), an official of the late Goryeo period; "*Donginjimun*" (Anthology of Poems of the Silla and Goryeo Literati) compiled by Choe, Hae (1287-1340); "Seolgok sigo" an Anthology of Poems by

Jeong, Po (1309-1347). There are also historical books published during the Goryeo dynasty: "*Samguk sagi*", "*Jewang ungi*", etc.

2. The Appearance of Movable Metal Type

2.1 Why Movable Metal Type?

During the Goryeo period, as the technique of woodblock printing was being upgraded to a large extent with the two-rounds of the Goryeo Daejanggyeong engraving projects and the production of various wood-block prints, printing culture was in its heyday. Then, why did movable metal type appear despite the flourishing woodblock printing culture?

The answer lies in the weaknesses of woodblock printing. First, it took too much time and expense to produce woodblocks for printing. Before making woodblocks, they had to be trimmed for engraving, and it also took too much time, expense, and human labor to engrave letters on the trimmed woodblocks. Even after the engraving was finished, it took a great deal of time, expense, and human labor to proof-read and correct them. In addition, since woodblocks were literally made of wood, they were prone to decay, warping, and fire.

Movable metal type, on the other hand, were more efficient in many ways, even though it required a sophisticated production technique and complex processes, compared to woodblock printing, which could only print one type of book with so many woodblocks engraved and had many other weaknesses. Movable metal type printing emerged due to the social demand for resolving such problems and letting the world know the status of Goryeo as a cultural powerhouse. Movable metal type printing is a technique to produce letters one by one with metal and typeset movable type pieces depending on the content of the book. Movable type was not only convenient, but also allowed other books to be printed with used movable type pieces. They were also not easily damaged and much more durable than woodblocks. From this point of view, movable metal type was technically superior to woodblock printing. It had so many advantages: the even and regular shapes of letters, a relatively fast process, the

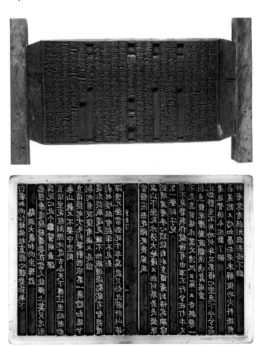

Woodblock and Movable Metal Type Printing Plate

reusability of type pieces which could be used to print other books, etc. The motivation to invent this new printing technique was to meet the demand of the time for more convenient, more practical, and faster printing.

2.2 The Background Behind the Appearance of Goryeo's Movable Metal Type Printing

In ancient times, when no letters existed, early humans used body language and gestures and sound to communicate and deliver information. As time went by, they evolved to use signs and drawings to record or convey messages. With the development of letters afterward, the means for recording and delivering information was changed into the form of literature, and a larger volume of literature was disseminated. The production of literature began with manual transcription for copying, then moved to woodblock printing, and movable type to publish books. The invention of movable metal type and movable metal type printing played an indispensable role in the transmission and development of civilization from ancient times.

There is almost no record that can definitely prove when movable metal type was invented and show the background of what led to its invention. However, assumptions can be made from records in literature that have been passed down over time.

Among various arguments about the time of Goryeo's invention of movable metal type, "before 1232 (the 19th year of King Gojong)" is accepted as the most convincing theory according to the postface of the original book that was included in *"Nammyeong Cheon hwasangsong jeungdoga"* (Song of Enlightenment with Commentaries by Buddhist monk Nammyeong, to be referred to as *"Jeungdoga"* hereafter), the woodblock-printed version of the book originally printed with movable metal type. There is another record about movable metal type during Goryeo: in *"Dongguk Isanggukjip"*, where it was written that "28 copies of *"Sangjeong yemun"* were printed with movable metal type and sent to several regional government offices for storage." The record was written by Lee, Gyu-bo on behalf of Choe Yi who ruled Jinyang area at that time, and since Choe Yi was appointed to rule the area in 1234 and Lee, Gyu-bo died in 1241, it could be inferred that Sangjeong yemun was printed sometime in between.

In addition to the two facts, there are other records to consider: 1) when China produced clay movable type in the early 11th century, the advantages of many techniques would have been introduced to Goryeo; 2) there are records that Goryeo already made metallic money during King Seongjong's time (960-997). Considering this, it could be inferred that Goryeo invented movable metal type no later than in the early 13th century, before the capital was moved to *Ganghwado*.

Printing books with movable metal type is possible only when several preconditions are met: the production of paper in large quantities, the production of ink suitable for movable metal type, movable metal type casting techniques, and skilled people. All of these conditions were already met and in practical use in Goryeo.

From its early days, Goryeo produced paper in large volumes. In 983 (the 2nd year of King Seongjong), each administrative office received and ran some land to buy paper, ink, writing brushes, and other tools to make a book, and paper-producing factories were built. Such records can be found in many parts of "*Goryeosa*" (History of Goryeo). There is also Chinese literature to show that paper made in Goryeo was exported to China and had a reputation for having excellent quality. Goryeo also had an agency that produced ink in large volumes to meet the demand for movable type printing and to export to China.

Concerning the movable metal type casting technique, Korea had had high quality metals from old times, and iron manufacturing technology was highly advanced in many provinces. The Silla dynasty had the technology to make huge Buddhist temple bells, such as the Bell of King Seongdeok in Gyeongju. The Goryeo dynasty also had techniques to make Buddhist temple bells, statues of the Buddha, metallic money, and various letters from Buddhist scriptures, which indicated that it met all the necessary conditions to cast movable metal type. The fact that the metallic money casting method was the same with the method to cast movable metal type also suggested that it would not be difficult to make movable metal type. Goryeo technicians who were skillful at producing money with molds were likely to invent molds for movable metal type as well as ink more appropriate for typography printing than woodblock printing.

At the same time, many of the woodblocks and the Buddhist literature on paper were destroyed and disappeared after several wars due to foreign invasion, and two civil wars during King Injong's reign caused more damage to books.

Considering the situation around the early and mid-12th century, book repositories and libraries were destroyed during several wars. To restore the destroyed libraries and become a cultural powerhouse, the publication of books became a top priority. Since China, the largest literature exporter back then, was in political and social chaos, it was difficult to bring books from China. Since there were almost no exchanges with China, Goryeo had to meet the cultural and intellectual demand by itself. However, there was a shortage of labor and time to publish books only with woodblocks.

This demonstrated that it was Goryeo's vitality, will, and techniques that enabled Goryeo to develop the world's first movable metal type. This situation facilitated the development of printing techniques and highlighted the need for movable metal type.

There are also sociocultural factors. Goryeo had strong educational and cultural policies, which resulted in a higher zeal for education and an increase of literature publication. In Goryeo, Silla's bone-rank-system-based aristocratic society centered on the king and high-ranking officials collapsed and the society was ruled by officials from indigenous forces of the region and social success came to depend on academic capabilities. In particular, the state-administered examination, which started from the mid-10th century, opened a wider path to success during Silla. With the stronger educational and cultural policies of the State, state-run educational institutions, such as Gukjagam in the state capital and Hyanggyo in provinces, were established. In particular, from the 11th to the early 12th century, the number of private schools established by retired high-ranking officials dramatically increased and came to outperform the national institutions.

Thanks to education promotion policy and a higher zeal for education, the demand for books grew at a rapid pace. Books printed in the capital were offered to the king or sent to provinces. An increasing amount of literature and woodblocks made in provinces were sent to the capital. The following shows such examples.

■ When Choe, Ho, Na, Ji-yeol, and others followed the king's order to newly publish and offer "Book of the Later Han," "Book of Han," and "Old Book of Tang," the king bestowed all of them with government posts. ("*Goryeosa*" vol. 6, February 25, 1042)

 ▪ When Biseoseong offered 70 newly published copies of "*Yegijeongeui*" and 40 copies of "*Mosijeongeui*," each copy was kept in the Eoseogak library and the rest were bestowed to officials. (*Goryeosa*" vol. 6, April 23, 1045)

The records shows that woodblocks engraved in provinces were offered to the King: a record of "Chungjumok offering 99 woodblocks for medical books including "*Cheonokjip*" (川玉集), "*Sanghannon*" (傷寒論), and "*Bonchogwalyo*" (本草括要) in 1058 (the 12th year of King Munjong)," Goryeosa vol. 8 Sep. 1, 1058; a record of "Anseodohobu offering 94 woodblocks for medical books including 73 woodblocks of "*Juhubang*" (肘後方), 11 woodblocks of "*Euiokjip*" (疑獄集), and 10 woodblocks of "*Cheonokjip*" (川玉集), and Gyeongsanbu offering 680 woodblocks of "*Suseo*" (隨書) in 1059, Goryeosa vol. 8 Feb. 9, 1059; and "Namwonbu offering 54 woodblocks of "*Samryedo*" (三禮圖) and 92 woodblocks of "*Songyeongjaseo*" (孫卿子書) in 1059," *Goryeosa* vol. 8 Apr. 16, 1059.

Goryeo was able to have a great deal of literature because it published in large amounts internally while importing many books from China. As the demand for literature grew, not only the existing woodblock printing but movable metal type printing started to be used to print literature.

Goryeo had a high zeal for education. The level of education and culture of Goryeo at that time was described in "*Goryeodogyeong*" (1124), written by an envoy from the Sung Dynasty of China. He considered Goryeo to be "a state with highly developed culture and civilization" and wrote his surprise about the facts that in Goryeo, there were many talented people and both academic study and education were advanced. For example, he vividly described the Goryeo people's zeal for education, "In Goryeo, the classical scholars were most highly evaluated among all occupations, so illiteracy was shameful in this country. Unmarried children made a group to go to teachers and learn from them, and when they grew older, they also made a group with friends to go to Buddhist temples to study. Low-ranking soldiers and little children also went to teachers and ask for their teaching."

Goryeo imported books from China to obtain information, then re-exported the information to China, playing the role of an information powerhouse. Considering that Goryeo had information from a variety of literature that could be compared to the Sung Dynasty, it must have been burdensome for Goryeo to depend sole on woodblock printing and transcribing for the domestic distribution of literature. It was because both transcribing and woodblock printing took too much time and expense. While China had a large population, Goryeo had a limited demand for literature mostly from the intellectual and ruling classes.

Therefore, it felt a strong necessity for movable metal type as it was most appropriate to produce a small number of books compared to woodblocks which was appropriate for mass production.

The agency exclusively responsible for the publication and storage of books continued to exist until the end of the Goryeo Dynasty. In March 1101 (the 5th year of King Sukjong), Seojeockpo (書籍鋪) was set in Gukjagam to store all the book editions and print and distribute them as the number of woodblocks stored in Biseoseong, a department responsible for books and documents, increased rapidly and a larger number of them were destroyed. King Munjong (reign period: 1046-1083) established the Seojeockjeom, an agency responsible for book-related administrative issues. In 1308 (the 1st year of King Chungseon), it was merged into the Yemun Chunchugwan (藝文春秋館) and was closed in 1391 (the 3rd year of King Gongyang). In 1392 (the 4th year of King Gongyang), it was re-established as the Seojeokwon to handle movable type casting and book printing. This was proven by the record in the section of the book control department in Goryeosa, where it is written: "During King Munjong's reign, the government structure was decided, and King Chungseon merged it (the department responsible for books) in Hallimwon (Academy of Letters), and then restored it. In the 3rd year of King Gongyang (1391), it was closed but in the 4th year of King Gongyang (1392) the Seojeockwon was established to take responsibility for movable type casting and book printing." It also showed that the Seojeokwon, on behalf of the Seojeokjeom, handled movable type production and publication at the end of Goryeo. This clearly shows that Goryeo had satisfied not only the technical conditions but also the sociocultural conditions for movable type printing.

III

Records about Books Printed with Movable Metal Type From Goryeo and *"Jikji"*

1. Records of Books Printed with Movable Metal Type

The creativity and excellence of Goryeo's movable metal type printing became more prominent when compared with those of China and Europe from the perspective of the world's printing history

Movable type printing in China started with clay movable type, invented by Bi Sheng (畢昇) between 1041 and 1048 during the Northern Song Dynasty (960-1127). This type was made by engraving letters on clay and burning them. The invention of clay movable type was meaningful in that it was the first movable type, but it could not be used practically because it was not durable and was easily broken. However, the attempt to make movable type to print books was highly evaluated and the concept as well as the process likely impacted the appearance of movable metal type during the later period of Goryeo.

Nonetheless, movable metal type printing was not very successful in China. During the reign of Emperors Hongzhi and Zhengde of the Ming dynasty (1488-1521), the private sector used movable metal type for printing, but the technique was very poor, the shape of characters was uneven, and the edges of the printing plates were not precise. Because the existing movable metal type print of China shows characteristics very similar to those of Korean print—the shape of movable type pieces, the matrix of characters, and the level of ink thickness and thinness, it was assumed that they were influenced by Korea.

During the Japanese invasions of Korea (1592–1598), Japan plundered a number of movable metal type pieces and printing tools as well as all kinds of literature from Joseon. In 1597, it made wooden movable type by imitating the movable metal type of Joseon to print many books, and by 1615, it succeeded in printing books with movable metal type, which allowed Japan to have a printing revolution even though the only method it had was woodblock printing by the end of the 16th century. Judging by these facts, Goryeo's movable metal type printing was clearly ahead of that of China and Japan, and the Korean people displayed their originality by continuously developing the technology. In this regard, Korea's movable metal type proves the creativity and superiority of the Korean culture and has left an important milestone in the printing history of Northeast Asia as well as the world.

Records in some literature prove that movable metal type was used for printing during the Goryeo dynasty. Together with such records, some of woodblock-printed versions of the books originally printed with movable metal type still exist. However, none of them provide detailed information on exactly when, where, why, and by whom the movable metal type was created. The following examples are the records related to the movable metal type printing of Goryeo from related records and literature that still exist.

1.1 Sangjeong yemun

The postface of Sangjeong yemun had a record about the movable metal type of Goryeo after the "*Nammyeongcheon hwasang songjeung-doga*" (南明泉和尚頌證道歌, sermons of Buddhist Priest Nam *Myeongcheon*). What was written in the postface was the first record that it was printed with movable metal type in Goryeo.

Sangjeong yemun is a book on present and past courtesies compiled by seventeen academic officials at the command of King Injong during his reign. The book itself has not been found yet. The record of printing it with movable metal type was in the article titled "Sinin Sangjeong Yemun Balmi"(新印詳定禮文跋尾), written by *Lee, Gyu-bo* on behalf of *Choe Yi* in the second volume of "*Dongguk isangguk*," a compilation of poetry and prose written by *Lee Gyu-bo*. "*Dongguk isanggukjip*" was 53 volumes in total, and the first compilation of 41 books were published before he died and the remaining 12 books—which contained what were not included in the first compilation—were published after his death. Only the first compilations were printed with movable metal type.

In the postface, the following was written: "It was difficult to refer to Sangjeong yemun complied by *Choi, Yoon-eui* (崔允儀) and others because the cover of the book was lost and the letters became faint as a long time had passed since its publication. After Choe, Chung-heon (1149-1219), father of Choe Yi, edited them and wrote two copies, he left one copy in the government office and the other at his house. However, the copy stored in the government building was lost when the national capital was moved to *Ganghwado* due to invasions by the Mongolians, and the only copy left was in *Choe, Yi's* possession. Therefore, 28 copies of 50 *Sangjeong yemun* printed with movable metal type were sent by them to several government offices to store and use."

Although it was not known exactly when *Sangjeong yemun* was printed with movable metal type, considering that *Choe, Yi* was appointed to *Jinyanghu* in 1234 (the 21st year of King Gojong) and *Lee, Gyu-bo* died in 1241, it could be assumed that it was published between 1234 and 1241.

1.2 Nammyeongcheon hwasangsong jeungdoga

This book is an anthology of 320 poems—each poem consists of three seven-character phrases—written by Buddhist monk *Nammyeong* as commentaries to "*Geungdoga*"(Songs of Enlightenment) originally written by Buddhist monk *Hyeungak* of the Tang dynasty. This book elaborated on the deep meaning of Geungdo (enlightenment). At the end of the extant woodblock-printed version of *Geungdoga*, there is a postface written by *Jinyanggong Choi Yi*. The following is the content of the postface.

"Since *Geungdoga* is an essential book in Buddhism, technicians were recruited and the books that were originally printed with movable metal type were engraved on woodblocks to pass them down for a long time. This is recorded by *Choe, Yi*, Jungseoryeong Jinyanggong, in the first part of September 1239 (… 於是募工 重彫鑄字本 以壽其傳焉 時己亥九月上旬中書令晉陽公崔怡謹誌)."

Here, "重彫" means "engraved on woodblocks again," "鑄字," "movable metal type pieces were cast" and "重彫鑄字本," "the book printed with movable metal type were attached to woodblocks for engraving." In other words, pages were separated from the book printed with movable metal type and attached to woodblocks, and characters on the pages were engraved to print the book again. This means that the remaining number of *Geungdoga* printed with metal type was small, so it was engraved on woodblocks to print more books.

Goryeo moved its capital to *Ganghwado* in 1232 (the 19th year of King Gojong), and *Choe, Yi* was appointed as *Jinyanggong* in 1234 (the 21st year of King Gojong). It was in 1239 (the 26th year of King Gojong) when the woodblock-printed version of *Geungdoga* was published.

It was assumed that *Geungdoga* was printed in *Gaeseong* before the capital was moved to *Ganghwado*. However, in contrast to the assumption, if movable metal type printing technology at that time was much more advanced than what is assumed now and was commonly used in the central area, it would be possible to cast movable metal type again in *Ganghwado* and print *Geungdoga* there. At the same time, it cannot be ruled out that there was a possibility of bringing movable metal type and technicians from Gaeseong to *Ganghwado*. Although the established theory is that *Geungdoga* would be printed in Gaeseong before the capital's relocation, it still requires further study. Nonetheless, if there is one thing known for sure, it would be the fact that movable metal type was already invented and used in the early 13th century or before.

Postface of *Geungdoga*(1239)

Woodblock-printed *Geungdoga* showed sophisticatedly engraved letters, and since the central government office published them with woodblocks by attaching the pages of the book original printed with movable metal type on them, they clearly displayed the characteristics of movable metal type printing. With only a few early records on movable metal type printing left today, *Geungdoga* has a very significant meaning in that it is the earliest record among extant records that tells us the timing and characteristics of movable metal type printing by the central government offices.

2. *Jikji*

"*Jikji*" is a book of teachings and sermons of Buddha and Buddhist sages, compiled by Baegun hwasang (白雲和尙, 1299-1375). The book, printed at Heungdeoksa temple on the outskirts of Cheongju in 1377, is the world's oldest extant movable metal type printed text. The size of the book is 24.6×17.0cm and it consisted of two volumes. No one knows where the first volume is, and only the 38-page second volume is extant. *Jikji* dramatically appeared at a book exhibition in Paris during the "International Book Year," and it turned out to be the oldest extant movable metal type print, which is 78 years ahead of Gutenberg's movable metal type.

Seokchan (釋璨) and Daljam (達湛), the disciples of Baegun hwasang, with offerings from the female priest Myodeok (妙德), printed it to disseminate their master's teachings to the world. The passage at the end of the book states that "it was printed with movable metal type at Heungdeoksa Temple on the outskirts of Cheongju in July, the 3rd year of King U (1377)."

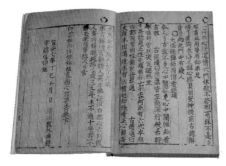

Postface of *Jikji*(1377)

In 1887, when Collin de Plancy (1853-1922) came to Korea as the first French Minister to Korea, he collected many Korean old books including *Jikji* and returned to France with his collections. In 1900, *Jikji* first appeared at the world's fair held in Paris. After that, *Jikji* was included in the fourth volume of "Korean Bibliography" written by Morris Courant, but it did not draw much attention back then. In 1911, Henri Vever, a French jeweler, bought *Jikji* for 180 francs at an auction held at Hotel Drouot. After his death, according to his wishes in his will, the book was donated to the National Library of France in 1952.

Dr. Park, Byung-seon
(December 23, 1972, The Joseon Ilbo)

Jikji cannot be discussed without mentioning Dr. Park Byung-seon. She started to work as a researcher at the National Library of France from 1967, and in the same year, she discovered *Jikji* among numerous library collections. After thorough investigation, it reappeared at an international book fair held in the National Library of France in Paris, under the sponsorship of UNESCO from May to October, 1972. At the fair, it was internationally certified that *Jikji* is the world's oldest extant book printed with metal type, which is ahead of Gutenberg's Bible.

After *Jikji* reappeared, the location of Heungdeoksa Temple, where the oldest movable metal type print was published, drew attention from the world. In October 1985, thirteen years later, the site where the old Heungdeoksa had been located was miraculously excavated in Uncheondong, Cheongju city, during a housing site development construction. Cheongju now has become a city that represents the printing culture of the world as the city that produced the world's oldest extant movable metal type printed book.

The name of the movable type used to print *Jikji* at Heungdeoksa temple in Cheongju is generally called "Heungdoeksa type". The temple also printed "Jabi Doryang Chambeop Jiphae" (慈悲道場懺法集解, a Collection of Commentaries on the Principles on Mercy and Ascetic Practices) with movable metal type. The fact that the temple had printed other books with movable metal type was known as the woodblock printed version of Jabi Doryang Chambeop Jiphae was found in Korea. *Jikji* and Jabi doryang chambeop jiphae prove that the temple in Cheongju printed books with movable metal type, and not only the capital but also local provinces widely used movable metal type for printing by the end of Goryeo. Heungdeoksa Temple played a meaningful role in that it kept Goryeo's movable metal type printing alive by casting movable metal type pieces and printing literature with them at a time when the central government's role in casing and printing with movable metal type was paralyzed due to the humiliating rule of the Yuan dynasty of China.

Korean Pavilion at the world's fair in 1900

This article has examined *Jikji*, the world's oldest extant book printed with movable metal type during the Goryeo dynasty, and other movable metal type printed books of the same period that are not extant but recorded in literature. The dynasty invented movable metal type at least around 1200 and printed literature with it. Although there are records about books printed with movable metal type prior to *Jikji*, which was printed in 1377, they have not been found yet. Recently, however, the actual movable type pieces, which are estimated to have been cast during the Goryeo dynasty, have been excavated and been under in-depth and thorough investigation.

Since *Jikji* is the actual book printed with movable metal type, it is the only material evidence that shows the level of printing technology during Goryeo, which invented movable metal type for the first time in the world. The fact that movable metal type printing, state-of-the art technology at the time, was used not only in the state capital but in local provinces including Cheongju also proves that Goryeo was an information and knowledge powerhouse, and its highly sophisticated culture was not limited to its capital but flourished across the country.

IV

Splendid Culture of Movable Type of Goryeo, Inherited by Joseon

Frequent foreign invasions and political and social confusion continued until the end of Goryeo. In 1392, *Yi, Seong-gye* founded the Joseon dynasty and became the first king. As highly educated kings reigned afterward, the dynasty became a cultural powerhouse and reached a peak in academic studies. Movable metal type pieces were more widely used to disseminate and penetrate studying and knowledge.

Joseon further developed the movable metal type printing that it inherited from Goryeo. The founder of Joseon inherited many systems from Goryeo—the official posts of the department responsible for printing books, for example, used the same name Seojeokwon, which was established in 1392 (the 4th year of King Gongyang), and followed most of Goryeo's organizational setups as they were.

In 1403 (the 3rd year of King Taejong), the *Jujaso* (type casting center) was established under *Seungjeongwon* (the Royal Secretariat during the Joseon Dynasty of Korea) as the new administrative office responsible for casting type pieces and publishing literature, following the example of *Sejeokwon* of Goryeo. Kings of many generations took casting movable metal type pieces and printing books seriously, and the number of Confucian students who were interested in further studying dramatically increased. As the short supply of literature caused difficulties in learning, various kinds of movable metal type were cast and used to print many more books.

Starting with Gyemi type, which was first cast in 1403 (the 3rd year of King Taejong), Joseon improved and developed its method of casting movable metal type. According to *Taejong Sillok* (the annals of King Taejong) and postface of Kwon, Geun, in 1403, *Jujaso* was established to print more books because Confucian students had difficulties studying due to the shortage of literature.

Due to the shortage of books in Korea, Confucian students could not read a wide range of books, and importing books from China was not easy because of the sea. On top of this, woodblocks with characters engraved on them were easily damaged, so they could not print all the books in the world. Concerned about the situation, in February of Gyemi year (1403) King Taejong ordered the casting of bronze movable type to print and distribute books. The expenses were covered by voluntary donations of bronze and iron from all the officials of the Royal Court. The metal type of Sijeon, Seojeon, and Jwassijeon stored in book repositories were used as basic characters, and casting was started from the 19th of the same month and the number of type pieces reached several hundred thousand in several months.

From the early days after its foundation, Joseon created over 35 kinds of movable metal type pieces including Gyemi type and Gapin type to print books. In particular, Gapin type, which was completed in 1434, was elaborate and letters printed with it were neat and tidy, revealing that the level of movable metal type printing in early Joseon was pretty high. The following list shows the type of movable metal type pieces cast during Joseon before and after Japanese invasions of Korea (1592–1598). The type pieces were named after the name of the year of the sexagenary cycle, the name of the book to print with it, and the name of the person who wrote the letter.

Movable Type before the Japanese Invasions of Korea

Gyemi type (癸未字, 1403), Gyeongja type (庚子字, 1420), Gapin type (甲寅字, 1434), Byeongjin type (丙辰字, 1436), Gyeongo type (庚午字, 1450), Eulhae type (乙亥字, 1455), Jeongchuk type (丁丑字, 1457), Muin type (戊寅字, 1458), Eulyu type (乙酉字, 1465), Gapjin type (甲辰字, 1484), Gyechuk type (癸丑字, 1493), Byeongja type (丙子字, 1516), Inryeok type (印曆字, 16 C), Gyeongjin type (庚辰字, 1580), Eulhaejae chegyeongseo type (乙亥字體經書字, around 1587)

Movable Type after the Japanese Invasions of Korea

Muo type (戊午字, 1618), Musin type (戊申字, 1668), Byeongjin yoaeeon type (丙辰倭諺字, 1676), Nakdonggye type (洛東契字, around 1673), Hyeonjong sillok type (顯宗實錄字, 1677), Choju hangu type (初鑄韓構字, around 1677), Jeonggi gyoseogwan inseoche type (前期校書館印書體字, before 1684), Wongjong type (元宗字, 1693), Hugi gyoseogwan inseoche type (後期校書館印書體字, before 1723), Yulgok jeonseoche type (栗谷全書字, 1749), Imjin type (壬辰字, 1772), Jeongyu type (丁酉字, 1772), Jaeju hangu type (再鑄韓構字, 1782), Choju jeongri type (初鑄整理字, 1795), Jeongrijache movable metal type (整理字體鐵活字, before 1800), Jeongsa type (全史字, 1816), Pilseoche movable metal type (筆書體鐵活字, early 1800), Jaeju seongri type (再鑄整理字, 1858)

After the *Jujaso* was established in 1403 (the 3rd year of King Taejong), several hundred thousand bronze movable type pieces (Gyemi type), both small and large characters combined, were cast to print books. It was 40 years ahead of Gutenberg's movable type in Germany. The dynasty enjoyed a flourishing civilization and culture when *Hunminjeongeum* (or *Hangul*, the Korean alphabet) was created during the reign of King Sejong.

King Sejong cast a number of movable type pieces including Gyeongja type and Gapin type by ceaselessly working to innovate printing tech-

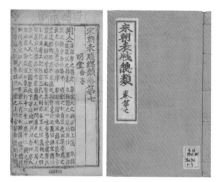

Songjo pyojeon chongnyu (Collection of Appeals and Letters to the Emperors of Song Dynasty), the first book printed using movable metal type print after *Jikji*, printed with *Gyemi* type

nology, and left many achievements by publishing scriptures on various subjects.

Gyeongja type was cast in 1420 because King Sejong wanted to improve the uneven and tough shape of Gyemi type.

In 1434, over 200,000 Gapin type pieces were newly created because its predecessor, Gyeongja type, was so dense that it was difficult to read. The type was top flight among Korea's metal type and the basis of Joseon's movable type. The shape of the type was elegant and beautiful and the type pieces themselves led to huge improvements in typesetting and printing capabilities. Gapin type was used for the longest period during Joseon to publish countless books, and was improved six times from its first creation in 1434 to the end of Joseon.

Byeongjin type was created in 1436 (the 18th year of King Sejong) because Gapin type was so detailed that it was hard to read. When publishing *Jachi tonggam gangmok*, a Chinese history book, bigger type pieces were used.

Gyeongo type was created by King Munjong in 1450, as he decided to melt down Gyeongja type, which used small letters and was not very efficient for recreating type with a typeface based on the handwriting of Prince Anpyeong. Eulhae type was created in 1455 when King Sejo dethroned King Danjong and came to the throne himself. The previous Gyeongo type, which was created by making typeface mimicking the handwriting of Prince Anpyeong, was melted down to make Eulhae type with a typeface based on the handwriting of Kang, Hee-an.

Eulyu type was created in 1465 (the 11th year of King Sejo) to print *Daebanggwang wongak sudara youigyeong* with a typeface based on the handwriting of Jeong, Nanjong. Gapjin type was created in 1484 (the 15th year of King Seongjong). To make this type, Eulyu type pieces were melted down to make bigger type pieces, and in the flowing year, small type pieces were cast. Over 300,000 big and small type pieces were created, and

Jachi tonggam printed with Gapin type

since they were used for over a hundred years, there are many extant books printed with them.

Hyeongjong sillok type consisted of around 40,000 newly cast type pieces and 35,000 metal type pieces purchased from a private organization named "Nakdonggye" to print "Hyeonjong Sillok" in 1677 (the 3rd year of Sukjong). They were used for some 190 years from the early period of King Sukjong to the early period of King Gojong.

Around 1677, Hangu type was personally made type by Kim, Seokju (金錫冑), son of Kim, Jwamyeong, a technician who cast Muo type— Gapin type was cast for six times during the Joseon period, and the Gapin type which was cast for the third time was named as Muo to avoid confusion. It was cast with a typeface based on the unique and attractive handwriting of Han, Gu (韓構), a master calligrapher of the time.

Gyoseogwan inseoche type, which was made at the Gyoseogwan by imitating the calligraphy style of the Ming dynasty of China, was cast two times. The first type was "Jeonggi gyoseogwan inseoche," cast in the early period of King Sukjong (before 1684) and the second, "Hugi gyoseogwan inseoche" was cast in the early period of King Gyeongjong (before 1723).

Wonjong type was bronze metal type cast in 1693 (the 19th year of

Sukjong) to print *Maengja eonhae* (Annotation to Mencius in *Hangul*) and *Maengja daemun*. It was cast based on the handwriting of Wonjong, father of King Injo. *Yulgok jeonseo* type was a bronze movable type personally created in 1749 (the 25th year of King Yeongjo) by Hong, Gyeheui with his disciples and acquaintances to print *"Yulgok seonsaeng jeonseo"* (The Complete Collection of Yulgok Seonsaeng's Writings) compiled by his teacher Lee, Jae (李縡).

Jeongri type refers to over 300,000 bronze movable type pieces cast in 1795 based on the typeface of Saengsaeng type (生生字, wooden movable type). After a fire at *Jujaso* burned all the pieces of Jeongyu type and Hangu type, they were re-cast in 1858, and named "Jaeju jeongri type."

Jeongrijache movable metal type was cast by the private sector at the end of King Jeongjo's reign (around 1798) and used by the end of the Joseon dynasty to print and distribute literature on various subjects including anthologies, family genealogy books, Confucian classics, medical books, fiction on royal history, and books on filial piety in the Seoul and Honam areas.

Pilseoche movable metal type was cast by the private sector in the early period of King Sunjo and was widely used for commercial printing including anthologies, family genealogy books, and general books from the period of King Sunjo to the King Gojong period.

After the creation of *Hangul, Hangul* movable metal type was made to be used alongside Chinese characters. Buddhist and Confucian scriptures, for which printing was led by the state, were translated into Korean and printed with *Hangul* movable metal type. They were also used to penetrate literature in the private sector by the late period of Joseon, influencing the fostering of knowledge among ordinary people.

Considering that Korea created *Hunminjeongeum*, which was recognized as the most logical and scientific letters in the world, and cast using *Hangul* movable metal type to print literature, Korea was a cultural powerhouse for both movable type and letters in the history of world civilization.

The kinds of *Hangul* movable metal type were those used in parallel with Gapin type—the first *Hangul* movable metal type, those used in parallel with Eulhaejache gyeongseoche type that was exclusively used to print Confucian scriptures such as the Four Books and Three Classics, those used in parallel with Eulyu type, those used in parallel with Ungak inseoche type, those used in parallel with Choju geongri type, and those used in parallel with Jeonsa type, all of which left a number of books printed with *Hangul* movable metal type.

Hangul movable metal type, used in parallel with Gapin type, was used to print *"Wolincheongangjigok"* and *"Seokbo Sangjeol"*. *Hangul* movable metal type holds significant meaning as it was the first metal type of its kind after the creation of *Hangul*.

Hangul movable metal type, used in parallel with Eulhae type, was used for Korean translations of Buddhist scriptures in 1461 and created to translate *"Neungeomgyeong"* (The Surangama Sutra, or the Sutra of the Heroic Ones) into Korean. Eulhaejache *gyeongseo Hangul* movable type was the first *Hangul* movable type used for the Korean translation of books written in Chinese characters including *Saseo eonhae* and *"Sohak eonhae"* (eonhae means the translation of Chinese characters into Korean).

Books printed with *Hangul* movable metal type pieces, which were mostly cast in central government agencies such as *Jujaso* or Gyoseogwan were sent to government and educational institutions including government offices in the provinces and Seowon and Hyanggyo and bestowed to individuals to celebrate the passing the

"Wolincheongangjigok" printed with *Hangul* movable type used in parallel with *Choju gapin* type

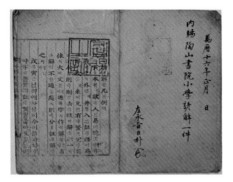

"Sohak eonhae" printed with *Eulhaejache gyeongseo Hangul* movable type

state-administered examination or appointments to official posts. In particular, books printed with movable metal type were distributed to local government offices, and then local governments used those books to engrave woodblocks to reproduce those books in large quantities to supply the populations of local areas. Many woodblock-printed versions of books printed with *Hangul* movable metal type still exist today.

V

Conclusion

In this paper, the culture of movable metal type printing in Goryeo was explained, along with the technical and sociocultural backgrounds of the creation of movable metal type in Goryeo and materials representing the woodblock printing of the Silla and Goryeo dynasties.

What proves the cultural superiority of the Korean people best is the publication and printing culture. It is safe to say that Korea has the status of a suzerain state in the world history of publishing and printing, considering "Mugujeonggwang Daedaranigyeong," the world's oldest woodblock printed material, and "*Jikji,*" the oldest extant book printed with movable metal type. There are more examples to prove the superiority of Korea's printing culture. During the Goryeo dynasty, massive projects to engrave and print Daejanggyeong were conducted two times based on the policy to promote Buddhism and its superb woodblock printing technique. For its part, Joseon had a great influence on the sharing and disseminating of knowledge. It continued to improve the movable metal type techniques it inherited from Goryeo and cast a variety Korean and Chinese character movable metal type pieces to produce literature together with woodblock printing.

Movable metal type printing was first started in Korea before Gutenberg developed movable metal type, which was considered the best human invention in the past 1,000 years. Even the extant *Jikji* proves that Korea's movable metal type was 78 years before Gutenberg's, and records in other literature suggest that the Korea's is over 200 years ahead of Gutenberg's.

Korea's movable metal type printing was not passed down nor did it develop into modern printing culture as Gutenberg's did. At the same time, it had obvious weaknesses: due to the limitation of movable metal type printing in its early forms, type pieces were not very sophisticated and as a result, the printed materials were not neat and clear. Nonetheless, Goryeo was the first in the world to invent movable metal type, something no other people had thought of. The Joseon dynasty after Goryeo further developed and used it for over 1,000 years until the end of the dynasty, while a variety of movable metal type pieces had been created under the initiative of the central government, which was unprecedented in the world history of printing culture. The fact that movable type pieces were continuously used to print diverse literature also proves the creativity and superiority of the Korean people.

As was illustrated in this paper, *Jikji*, the oldest extant book printed with movable metal type, is housed in the National Library of France and there are other extant records of literature printed with over 35 kinds of movable metal type including Gyemi type, Gapin type, and Gyeongja type, which were created by Joseon from the beginning of the dynasty.

Printing technology allowed mankind to move away from the oral transmission to widely share information and disseminate knowledge, which had a huge impact on the development of human culture. In this regard, it was a great achievement to invent movable metal type for the first time in the world.

The movable metal type printing of Goryeo had a profound impact on the development of printing culture in Korea. Joseon, which inherited printing techniques with movable metal type from Goryeo, printed and distributed all kinds of literature from history books, educational books, scriptures, and technical books through the central government. Each province reproduced over several hundred woodblock-printed versions of books printed with movable metal type. Such reproduced books were widely distributed into various classes including ordinary citizens and women.

In conclusion, Goryeo's invention of movable metal type and its movable metal type printing culture resulted in the continuous development of printing technology with movable metal type during the Joseon dynasty and impacted the modern printing history of Korea. The invention allowed the production and distribution of literature as well as the sharing of knowledge and information, thereby enlightening the general public. At the same time, it was the invention of movable metal type and its potential that allowed Korea to become one of the world's greatest cultural powers with highly advanced cellphone, semiconductor, IT, and internet technology.

References

Cheon, Hye-bong *"Book Printing History of Korea"*. Seoul: Bumwoosa, 1990.

Park, Byeong-seon *"Printing in Korea—from Origination to 1910"* Cheongju: Cheongju Early Printing Museum, 2005.

Nam, Gweon-heui *"Study of Recording Culture During the Goryeo Dynasty"* Cheongju: Cheongju Early Printing Museum, 2002.

Nam, Gweon-heui et al. *"Investigative Study on Original Text of Jikji, Housed in the National Library of France"* Journal of the Institute of Bibliography, 35th edition (2006)

Cheongju Early Printing Museum, *"Footprints of Jikji and Movable Metal Type"* Cheongju: Cheongju Early Printing Museum, 2002.

Kim, Doo-jong *"History of Korea's Printing Technology"* Seoul: Tamgudang, 1974.

Nam, Yoon-seong "The Meaning in Human History of Korea, the Inventor of Movable Metal Type and Jikji, the Memory of the World," "Journal of Korea Multimedia Society" 16 (2012), pp.1-9

Nam, Yoon-seong *"Proposal to Korea, the Inventor of Movable Metal Type and for Globalization of Jikji"* Journal of Hoseo Culture" 25 (2016), pp.59-72

Lee, Hee-jae *"Baegun hwasang chorok buljo jikjisimcheyojeol and Movable Type Printing Culture in Early Joseon"* Journal of the Institute of Bibliography, 28 (2004), pp.99-136

Park, Hee, *"The Meaning of Jikji in the History of Civilization and Visions for the Jikji Culture"* "Journal of Hoseo Culture" 24 (2015), pp.63-90.

Park, Mun-yeol *"The Modern Meaning of Buljo jikjisimcheyojeol, Printing of Goryeo's Movable Metal Type"* Journal of the Institute of Bibliography, 17 (1999), pp.125-154.

National Institute of Korean History, Edition of Association Française pour l'Etude de la Corée, Collected Journals for Symposium in Commemoration of 12th Anniversary of the French-Korean Relationship, 2006.

Lee, Se-yeol *"In-depth Study on Detailed Account of How Jikji Went to France"* Seowon University Lifelong Education Center, 2005.

The *Jikji* and the 42-line Bible
Focusing on the Invention of Printing
Technology in Asia and Europe and Its Impact on Society

Choi, Kaungeun

HK Research Professor, Institute of Humanities, Yonsei University

I

Introduction

The argument that the invention of printing technology put an end to the Middle Ages and laid the foundation for the beginning of modern times has been widely accepted in Europe. This is because it was a revolutionary event that created a driving force for the transformation of the outdated social system by disseminating knowledge and information, while paving the way for the age of the Reformation, Enlightenment, and Information. With the 42-line Bible, or the Gutenberg Bible, Europe changed from an era of manual transcription to one of typography, entering into a new period of information sharing in earnest. From this perspective, it is safe to say that the invention of printing technology was the first step to opening up the era of capitalism, information, and globalization that exists today.

In Asia, Korea invented movable metal type, a scientific duplication method, and possesses "*Baegun hwasang chorok buljo jikjisimcheyojeol[1]*" (the second volume of "Anthology of Great Buddhist Priests' Zen Teachings), the world's oldest existing book printed by movable

1) To be referred as "*Jikji*" hereafter

metal type. The *Jikji*, which was printed at Heungdeoksa temple in 1377, is the world's oldest metal print book that exists now as it was printed over 70 years before the Gutenberg's 42-line Bible that was printed in 1450[2]. The *Jikji*, however, had been forgotten for a long time and was neglected by those who study movable type printing technology. This quotation by Audin represents the misunderstanding that many Europeans have.

"It is interesting to confirm that movable type printing was invented almost at the same time in Korea and Rhine land, two regions at both ends of the northern hemisphere where building a direct relationship in a short period was unthinkable... The two inventions, without doubt, took place almost concurrently and was comparable to the society which was at the heart of changes.[3]"

Audin pointed out in his book that social desire, full of movement for changes in both Asia and Europe, was the driving force that led to the invention of printing technology. Yet, the social desire of Korea was different from that of Europe. Because Korea was experiencing rapid changes due to the change of dynasty, what it wanted from

---

2) In the colophon of the "*Jikji*", the time and place of its publication were listed as: "It was printed by movable metal type at the Heungdeoksa Temple outskirt of Cheongjumok in July 1377."
3) Maurice Audin, Histoire de l'imprimerie, Paris, A. et J. Picard, 1972, p 31.

metal movable typography was social stability while Europe desired social changes from it. On top of this, the time he mentioned—the regime of King Sejong the Great—was not the time of its inception but the time when movable metal type printing, which was invented at the end of the Goryeo dynasty, reached its peak after continuous improvement and development.

Misunderstandings like Audin's were rather common until the early 1970s, and his book was published in 1972. Interestingly, it was also 1972, when the "*Jikji*," which had been owned by the National Library of France, dramatically appeared at a book exhibition in Paris during the "International Book Year." As a result, 1972 was recorded as the first year when Korea's metal movable typography newly appeared in the history of printing and books[4]. Moreover, it is true that Korea's movable metal type printing technology, which is being accepted as the "first" of its kind by international academics, has had its importance called into questioned in terms of its socio-cultural role, compared with Gutenberg's printing technology that triggered rapid social transformation. As pointed out by Al Gore, the then vice-pres-

---

4) Since then, Koreans worked hard to make *Jikji* recognized as the world's first movable metal type printed book. Their thirty-year-long efforts were in the inscription of Jikji on the UNESCO Memory of World Register in 2004, earning international recognition. However, not a small number of Western scholars still think "Gyemi type," which was cast in 1403 (the third year of King Taejong) as Korea's first metal movable type, while a significant number of textbooks in the world describe Gutenberg as the "first inventor."

ident of the US, at the Information Society Conference in Brussels, Belgium in 1995[5], Korea's metal movable typography was deemed to have failed as a driving force for social reform led by the spread of information. It is safe to say that the remarks by Lee, O-young, a South Korean critic and novelist—saying that although Korea possessed outstanding metallurgy, ink production skills, and printing technique using movable metal type as well as paper manufacturing skills that were ahead of Europe, it failed to achieve modernization into an industrial economy or the social reform that Europe had achieved[6]—is a universal view into how European scholars felt about Korea's movable metal typography. From this point of view, the invention of typography in Korea, unlike in Europe, was not a revolutionary event that had an absolute impact on human culture and it only had insignificant socio-cultural ripple effects that were limited to the ruling class.

However, it should be pointed out that such analyses were made customarily while overlooking the obvious fact that typographies in Asia and Europe were invented in different socio-cultural contexts and demands and underwent different courses of development. As a result, they do not reflect the thorough investigation into the content

5) The Information Society Conference, remarks by Vice President Al Gore, Brussels, Belgium, February 25, 1995.
6) Lee, O-young "What Is Behind the Desire for Printing—the Printing Culture in the East and the West" The 3rd International Symposium on Printing and Publishing Culture (2000), The Organizing Committee of Cheongju Printing and Publication Exposition., P.3

of the desire for printing technology, the context in which the desire appeared and the specific circumstances. This paper will analyze the socio-cultural factors behind the development of typography in Asia and Europe to prove that it satisfied the desire for new technology in the East as well as in the West at the time when typography was invented and developed and fully played its own role in the respective societies. If the printing technology played different roles and functioned differently in two different worlds, it was because each culture had different demands and values from the invention. Before making a judgement on whether or not a technology played an efficient role in the maintenance and development of a society, the diversity of each society and culture should be recognized. Any attempt to deem the technology in a different society a success or failure by the criteria of another society and its culture criteria is very risky. This understanding should be the prerequisite for any judgement on the influence of the printing technology in Asia and Europe.

II

Duplication Methods prior to the Movable Metal Typography

1. The Culture of Transcription in Europe

In medieval Europe, duplication techniques using woodblocks and copperplates were already being used before the invention of the movable metal typography, but manual transcription was most widely used for duplication. In the early Middle Ages, when papyrus scrolls were gradually being replaced by parchment codices, letters stopped being used outside monasteries, and only the clergy started keeping and supplying information in words. The motto, "a monastery without a room for transcription is the same as a castle without an armory[7]," well captures the characteristics of monasteries, the hub of the letter culture during the Middle Ages. The network connecting the Roman Catholic Church with monasteries firmly ruled medieval Europe by keeping and supplying letters.

In the early Medieval period, Catholic monks were the only users of letter; the Creation in the Bible was done by the Word of God, and

---

7) Claustrum sine armario est quasi castrum sine armamentario.

words were letters[8]. Since Christianity was the religion with the Bible, the sacred book, it was natural to admire those who were responsible for duplicating letters. In a society where most of the population was illiterate, members of the clergy who knew letters enjoyed privileges, and their transcribing work was described as a sacred action. As clergymen were engrossed in duplicating transcriptions, the supply of parchment ran low and parchment already used once was frequently reused. It was transcription on recycled parchment that invited the birth and revival of the medieval Renaissance after the discovery of numerous ancient texts. During the re-transcription process, however, a number of original ancient text went missing because the original text was often discarded after transcription.

In the later period of the Middle Ages, the culture of transcription was in full bloom with the increased demand for texts and the supply of paper. Professional transcription workshops outside monasteries mushroomed. Patronage was need to produce expensive manuscripts because manuscript materials were exorbitantly priced and the livelihoods of transcribers need to be protected for the two years they would spend on transcribing a single codex.

During the Middle Ages, a manuscript was made based on an order.

---

8) "In the beginning was the Word, and the Word was with God, and the Word was God"(John 1:1).

"Art in the Middle Ages was order-based art in essence... All the pieces of art at churches were created based on orders[9]." If the concept of copyright was applied in manuscript production, it would be totally wrong to regard the orderer of a manuscript as the copyright holder in the Middle Ages. Names of transcribers were not known while those of orderers and patrons were back then. "Actions of patrons had to be followed by their names. This was so they would be remembered and those who came after them could pray for their soul for a long time[10]."

Paper, which was invented in China and brought into Europe by the Saracens, catalyzed the boom of the transcription culture. Medieval Europeans needed more manuscript books due to the cheap supply of transcription materials thanks to the introduction of paper, the growth of the reading population through the invention and spread of eyeglasses[11], and the increase of those using letters after the establishment of universities and the development of administrative organizations. This led to active commercial transactions over manuscripts produced outside monasteries. In the Holy Roman Empire (Germany), the shops of manuscript dealers were easily seen in

---

9) Bergmann, Ulrike. PRIOR OMNIBUS AUTOR - an höchster Stelle aber steht der Stifter. In: *Ornamenta ecclesiae(1985)*, S.117-148, p. 117.
10) Ibid., p. 145.
11) Eye glasses were invented in Venice or Firenze in 1284.

large markets or trans-regional commercial Messes at the end of the Middle Ages. At large events such as the Council of Konstanz (1414-1418) or the Oecumenical Council of Basel (1431-1449), book markets were held, and bureaucrats from the Vatican and the states and learned humanists used these markets. The Frankfurt Messe near the Rhine, which had already been established as "the most important international market in Europe[12]" in the 13th century, became specialized into the Frankfurt Book Messe by the mid-15th century thanks to the boom of manuscript transactions and typography which began in neighboring Mainz. A group of priests who led the culture of transcription in the late Middle Ages that was named the Brethren of the Common Life, a layperson organization formed in the Netherlands in 1386, sold manuscripts to make a living.

The most well-known transcriber was Diebold Lauber (?-1471), a teacher from Hagenau in Elsass. Between 1425 and 1467, he supplied manuscripts produced in his transcription workshop to regions near the Rhine, Franken, and Switzerland. He did not make expensive illustrated parchment codices, instead he made paper manuscripts with text in the transcribers' mother languages and with colored drawings through the division of labor between transcribers and illustrators.

---

12) Kapp, Friedrich: *Geschichte des Deutschen Buchhandels. Band 1: Geschichte des Deutschen Buchhandels bis in das siebzehnte Jahrhundert*, Verlag des Börsenvereins der Deutschen Buchhändler, Leipzig 1886 (Reprint), p. 448.

He practiced the modern market economy principle by selling pre-made manuscripts instead of custom-made ones.

Lauber, who ran a transcription workshop and was a kind of publisher, produced manuscripts that encompassed religious and secular salvation literature, literature for amusement, and pragmatic literature. He advertised his manuscript series in a one-page flyer as follows: "All the books that people want—whether big or small, religious or secular—you can find one through Diebold Lauber, the master artisan of transcription from Hagenau[13].

There is no definitive evidence for other transcription workshops in Europe

Illustration put in the "Story Bible" produced at Lauber's workshop, housed in the Mainz City Library

13) Wittmann, R., *Geschichte des deutschen Buchhandels*. 3.Aufl., München 2011, p. 20.

in the late Middle Ages. It was presumed that not a small number of wage-earning transcribers existed in large commercial or university cities. In such regions, transcription for transaction or administration was a must, and the citizenship classes—such as lawyers, medical scientists, business magnates, and members of city councils—were growing more interested in reading and possessing manuscripts in line with progressive social and cultural subdivisions. As reading become secular, it also promoted the gradual commercialization of books. In Europe, even before books could be duplicated by machines, they became products for transaction and consumption[14].

2. Woodblock Printing in Korea

Before the invention of printing technology, transcription also was the tool for Asia to disseminate and store knowledge and information, as in Europe. Transcription, however, always entailed the risk of misspelling and omissions and the original texts was exposed to the risk of being manipulated depending on the intent of the transcribers. The technological advancement and growing demand for books called for the invention of technology for printing. After the early stage of engraving on stones and bones, duplication technology in Asia appeared in the form of woodblock printing.

14) Schmidt-Künsemüller, Fr. A., Gutenbergs Schritt in die Technik. In: H. Widmann(Hg.), *Der gegenwärtige Stand der Gutenberg-Forschung(1972)*, p.124.

In Europe, woodblock printing was also used for about 100 years from the early 15th century after the printing method, together with paper, was brought from Asia. In Europe, however, the infrastructure for transcription, such as transcribers and transcription workshops, was already established at that time. This made it difficult for woodblock printing, which was imported from the East, to replace transcription. Moreover, the invention of movable metal type shortly after led to woodblock printing being used in a limited way to duplicate short texts explaining illustrations. Nonetheless, the importance of woodblock printing in Asian printing culture should not be underestimated because it was not technology that needed to be improved and replaced by movable metal type. It survived the invention of movable metal type and coexisted with and complemented movable metal type until the late 19th century. In particular, it is noteworthy that it was woodblock printing technology that played an important role in the massive duplication and exoteric dissemination of knowledge in Korea and in Asia. Woodblock printing was first used in the 7th century, and it had a long tradition of over 500 years before movable metal type was invented. "Woodblock printing was not the technology that had to be replaced while movable metal type printing was the technology for mass printing without a need for improvement. If any attempt to improve the technique for mass printing was made, it must be woodblock printing that the East Asian society would try to improve[15]." For instance, it was known that 100 to 300 copies were printed by movable metal type while woodblock printing was used for 300 to 1,000 copies during the reign of King Sejong the Great[16]. Considering that the average number of printed books in Europe in the 1500s was around 1,000[17], the number of copies for a single publication in Europe was not much different from the largest number of printed copies during the Joseon dynasty[18]. As such, the printing system in Korea was maintained in the form of a dual system of woodblock printing and movable metal type from the 13th century[19] to the end of the 19th century.

At the same time, woodblock printing maintained spiritual value in

15) Nam, Young "*Reconsideration on the History before and after the Development of the Movable Metal Type Printing—from "Superiority or Inferiority of the Technology to Cultural Diversity*" "Journal of Chung-Ang Historical Studies" 29th issue (2009), p. 27
16) Son, Bo-gi "*Printing and Publication during the King Sejong period*" King Sejong the Great Memorial Society, 1986. p, 42-64.
17) Wittmann, R., *Geschichte des deutschen Buchhandels.* 3.Aufl., München 2011, p. 27.
18) Nam, Young "*Reconsideration on the History before and after the Development of the Movable Metal Type Printing—from "Superiority or Inferiority of the Technology to Cultural Diversity*" "Journal of Chung-Ang Historical Studies" 29th issue (2009), pp. 15.
19) Unlike the West, the inventor of Korea's movable metal type and the first movable metal type printed material is not known. Though *Jikji* was printed in 1377, there are a number of records that indicate movable metal type printed materials before *Jikji*. What indicates it most clearly is "*Sangjeong yemun*" in "*Dongguk Isanggukjip*," but since the book itself has not been found, it has not internationally recognized. Based on the records in and actual printed materials "*Dongguk Isanggukjip*," "*Jungdoga*," "*Sambongjib*," and "*Goryeosa*," it is certain that movable metal type was invented before the 1230s in Korea. Nonetheless, since it is *Jikji* that is the first printed material that exist now, the discussion is to be limited to 1377, the year when *Jikji* was printed, and afterward. Cheon Hye-bong "*Korean Bibliography Studies*" Seoul: Minumsa, 1997. p.255-267.

Mugujeonggwang Daedaranigyeong

East Asia, which was totally differently from that of Europe. The act of making woodblocks and engraving letters on them held an ascetic importance. *"Mugujeonggwang Daedaranigyeong"*—a sutra (Buddhist canonical scripture) translated and printed with woodblocks in the mid-8th century—which was found inside Seokgatap (a stone pagoda) at the Bulguksa Temple in Gyeongju, was a woodblock-printed text that was printed in 751, before the pagoda was built. Instead of distributing and spreading the copies printed by woodblocks on which Chinese characters were engraved with great difficulty, Korean ancestors opted for putting them inside the pagoda to pass it on to future generations.

Even the primary purpose of *Palman Daejanggyeong* ("Eighty-Thousand Tripiṭaka" or the Tripiṭaka Koreana—a Korean collection of the Tripiṭaka (Buddhist scriptures and the Sanskrit word for "three baskets") carved onto 81,258 wooden printing blocks in the 13th century), which represents the printing culture of Korea, was not printing nor the production of duplications. The two large-scale Tripitaka woodblock carving projects began out of a religious prayer to save the country from foreign invasions with the help of Buddha rather than to print and publish books. Faced with a national crisis, the Goryeo people started the large-scale projects believing that carving on over 84,000 woodblocks itself was meaningful. The Tripiṭaka Koreana, currently housed in *Haeinsa* Temple, was the largest and oldest set of woodblocks in the world. The enormous collection has been perfectly managed and preserved until today. The Korean Tripitaka collection places significant meaning in the woodblocks themselves, rather than in the form of books printed in paper. Its central concept did not lie in duplication, which is widely accepted as natural nowadays. This shows that printing in Korea had a meaning far different from the concept of the West—mass production and the public dissemination of information.

At the time Gutenberg invented movable metal type printing, woodblock printing in East Asia was the technology that fully satisfied the needs of the society in terms of demand. On the other hand, woodblock printing had just begun to be used in Europe and was not a cultural tradition that should be preserved. At the same time, Europe required the means for mass printing to meet the growing social demand for reading. As a result, metal movable typography came to be widely used to satisfy the needs of society—the mass production and commercialization of books. In Korea, on the contrary, where woodblock printing functioned as a means for mass duplication, metal movable printing technology was developed toward satisfying the social desire that emphasized the spiritual meaning of printing. This illustrates that printing technology was developed toward different directions in the East and the West with different goals.

III

The Socio-cultural Background of the "42-line Bible" and the "*Jikji*" Printing

1. Demand and Profits

Around 1400s, the introduction of paper[20] expanded the use of letters in Europe. At the end of the 14th century, paper was sold at one sixth of the price of parchment and it made the standardization of the form of books and planning a life possible. That is why the first texts written on paper were secular and ordinary practical texts, such as letters, ledgers, transaction reports, court records, and city-related books. Since paper could be produced, stored, and kept in quantity unlike parchment, the introduction of paper changed the political and economic structure. This means that the early capitalist economy—paper bills, contract documents, market news, and documents for closing accounts in transactions—could be materialized with the help of paper. As a result, transcribing work was done more outside the network connecting churches and monasteries while being more

20) Concerning paper production factories in Europe, they were established in 1276 in Italy; in 1348 in France; and in 1389 in Germany. (Febvre, Lucien/Henri Martin. *L'apparition du Livre*. Paris, 1958).

specialized and complicated by the growing economic demand. Depending on various compositions of the transcribing process, independent workshops started to appear.

In cities, which rapidly increased from the mid-Medieval period, the cultural demand for writing grew strongly. In the 1400s, writers in cities were involved in various occupations and in particular, had legal knowledge or other commensurate knowledge. They not only wrote and recorded documents related to public offices and legal issues, but were also involved in resolving various tasks related to writing as "*homo litteratus* (human who use letters)," such as notaries, officials, protocol writers, members of diplomatic delegation, witnesses, and legal advisers to high-ranking officials.

The increased use of letters outside monasteries was related to new purposes and conditions. Since the early 15th century, the "publicness" of the early citizenship classes required members of city councils to have perfect writing and reading competencies. Additionally, the new reading population yearning for secular literature mushroomed in many areas. The urban bourgeois who learned letters was a case in point. Lawyers, layman court advisers, state officials, as well as wealthy merchants and citizens all needed books of not only their own disciplines including law, politics, and science but other themes such as literature, didactic morality, and the heroic episodes of knights.

The education of the laity, which grew after mendicant orders started their activities in the 13th century, gained momentum from the secularization of the church and the expansion of schools and universities at the end of the 14th century, and other players, along with the church—lords or cities— became more involved in education. City libraries and huge studies of wealthy book collectors since the end of the 14th century have remained until today. "Vocabularius Ex quo," a Latin-German dictionary, which was essential for self-studying and had been passed down in the form of manual transcript—there were 280 copies in the 15th century, was popular enough to be printed and published 48 times by 1505.

Around 1400, many small-sized private schools were established. They were generally operated by guilds of writing and reading masters under the supervision of city councils. Universities, which were first established in Italy and France in the 12th and 13th centuries, were also established in Germany in the mid-14th century. They were established in Prague (1348), Vienna (1365), and Heidelberg (1386), and in particular, universities were established concurrently with the foundation of cities in Cologne (1388) and Erfurt (1389). After 1400, urban authorities built university buildings outside the demesnes of churches and monasteries, and a large number of teachers belonged to the middle class of the 15th century. By the end of the 15th century, the aristocracies and urban noble families finally started to have interests in academic refinement. The development of libraries originated from

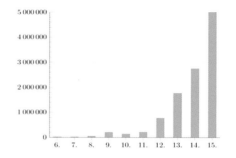

The number of manual transcriptions produced in Europe from the 6th to the 15th century

the occupation of "*stationarius*" (stationed personnel) at universities. They were responsible for the duplication and proofreading of study books and, in the 15th century, they became involved in the checking out of books.

Professors and students needed textbooks for lectures, and libraries were built inside universities to meet the demand for transcribers. Professional artisans composed of scriveners and book-seller guilds were employed by universities to write academic textbooks. As a growing number of universities were established, learning and education gradually left the domain of the church to be "secularized," triggering the exponential growth of letter users.

During the century before Gutenberg printed "*Vulgate*" or the 42-line Bible, many historical situations unfolded in Europe to make the invention of printing technology inevitable in many ways: paper was introduced, writing workshops flourished, the invention and supply of eyeglasses for reading increased the reading population, and primary users of letters expanded from the clergy to secular people in cities and administration offices. In addition, universities, which started to be established in the 13th century, brought about the expansion of reading classes.

At that time, Europe was enjoying the so-called "the golden age for the culture of transcription." The general public felt thirsty for books. An increased supply of paper was waiting for the invention of book printing technology. In the early 15th century, there was prevalent demand for methods to duplicate books in Europe, and arguments that they invented the printing press was frequently made. For example, France argued that Procopius Waldvogel first taught copying technology between 1444 and 1446 based on a document found in Avignon. The series of arguments—many countries argued that their nationals invented printing technology—in the 15th century indirectly demonstrated how desperately Europe wanted a book duplication method.

Gutenberg was also looking for a way to print Bibles in quantity in order to make money. It is generally known that printing requires more initial capital than any other business because of paper, parchment, ink, and payroll costs. He borrowed his initial capital from Johannes Fust. The investor was involved in many other areas of Gutenberg's business other than finance, and his colleague Peter Schöffer also actively joined his business because of his passion for the invention. This series of facts, known from Helmasperger's Notarial Instrument

(*Helmaspergerschen Notariatsinstrument*)[21], indirectly proves how lucrative the mass duplication of the Bible was at that time. Like all the other inventions, the surging demand and the desperate need ultimately led to the actual invention. In conclusion, the invention of book-printing technology in Europe was not "God's present

The single-parchment Helmaspergerschen Notariatsinstrument, Housed in the Göttingen Library

---

21) Füssel, Stephan. *Kommentar zu Leben und Werk von Johannes Gutenberg, zum Bibeldruck, den Besonderheiten des Göttinger Exemplars, dem "Göttinger Musterbuch" und dem "Helmaspergerschen Notariatsinstrument."*Taschen : Köln, 2018, p. 55.

from the heaven[22])," but the inevitable product of the demand of the time when transcription culture reached its peak and the rapid advancement of the technology was possible due to the Pan-European market starving for printed materials as well as the commercial minds of early printers.

2. Records and Education

Reproduction technologies before metal movable typography—ceramic movable type and woodblock printing technology, for example—were first invented in China. Ceramic movable type failed to be widely used due to its critical weakness of being fragile, while woodblock printing technology fulfilled the original intention of mass printing over a long period of time. It was Korea that introduced non-metal movable type printing technology from China to develop the metal movable type and succeeded in using it for practical purposes. If books were to be printed by the movable metal type, it was essential to have casting technology, quality paper, and ink sticks suitable for printing. The accumulation of these technologies as well as the demand for books were the socio-cultural driving force for the inven-

---

22) The illustration in the opening page on *Histoire de l'Origine et des Premiers Progrès de l'Imprimerie* by Prosper Marchand described the spirit of typography is coming down from the Heaven under the protection of Minerva and Mercurius, incidcating that printing technology is God's present from the heaven (Eisenstein, Elizabeth. *The Printing Revolution in Early Modern Europe*, Cambridge University Press, 1983)

tion of metal movable typography. At the end of the Goryeo dynasty, all of the above-mentioned conditions were met in Korea[23].

It was the Buddhist community that created the social demand for movable metal type printing technology at the end of Goryeo dynasty. At that time, there was a constant demand for Buddhist books, as it had been settled as the dominant ideology of Korea for over a thousand years. On top of this, "Buddhism had to find a way for sweeping reforms as it was under fierce attack by neo-Confucianism, the new study at that time, and its status was on the verge of crisis. Around the time when the *Jikji* was printed, Buddhism had lost a large part of its status as the dominant ideology of the state as it went through stages of political and social confusion—the period of the Goryeo military regime and of Mongol (Yuan) intervention, as well as criticism by neo-Confucianism." As a result, the Buddhist community sought restoration through diverse responses and underwent many drastic changes[24]. In a bid to tackle the difficulties facing it, the community sought various solutions, and the publication of the *Jikji* should be understood in this context. The *Jikji* was the so-called Bud-

23) One distinctive difference between Europe and Korea is that the existence of a market to trade books is not presumed as a prerequisite for the development of typography in Korea. The demand referred here does not mean a possibility of trading books in the market. This was because printing with movable metal type in Korea took place in a form of "national projects" to lay the foundation for the state
24) *"Traces of Jikji and Korean Movable Metal Types"* Cheongju Early Printing Museum, 2002. P. 66

dhist book for education, which contained a collection of excerpts from the analects of the most revered Buddhist monks' *Zen* teachings that would be helpful for many Buddhist monks[25]. According to the preface of the woodblock printed copy, written by Lee, Seak (1328-1396), Baegun (1299-1374, a Buddhist monk) inherited his Buddhism from a Zen master named Seokok (1272-1352) who gave Baegun a book titled "*Buljo Jikjisimcheyojeol*" that he wrote himself. After Baegun returned from China, he read and valued the book[26]. Baegun abstracted some contents from it and enlarged many parts into a book in two volumes and annotated it for compilations. The book, printed with movable metal type by Baegun's disciples after his death, was the "*Jikji.*" The original text of the *Jikji* was the writings of his late revered master in the only book in Korea. Baegun was cited as one of the three greatest Buddhist priests at the end of the Goryeo dynasty and had a profound influence on the Buddhist community. Considering that Buddhism could not be isolated from politics[27], as

---

25) As the title Jikji itself indicates, the book talks about an enlightenment from the phrase of "*Jikji insim gyungseong seongbul.*" "to see the heart straight of people's heart to find the true nature of Buddha and become a being like Buddha"

26) "*Traces of Jikji and Korean Movable Metal Types*" Cheongju Early Printing Museum, 2002. p, 27-28

27) According to the publication information, *Jikji* could be printed thanks to the offerings of female priest Myodeok. There are little records existing about her, but according to "*Myodeok Gyecheop*" and the last record of the volume 74 of "*Dongmunseon,*" she is portrayed as a wealthy individual who made many offerings to Buddhist projects. Some tried to connect her with the Royal family by considering her as the wife of Jeongangun, but there is no concrete evidence to support such arguments. Lee, Se-yeol "*The Study on the Jikji and Female Priest Myodeok*" Jungwon Culture Study Series Vol.4 No.1 (2000)

it was the state religion, it could be inferred that the invention of printing with movable metal type was developed in close relations with the political circles of the dynasty.

In the Joseon dynasty after Goryeo, metal movable typography played an instrumental role in resolving the pressing task of the accurate dissemination of neo-Confucianism, the dominant ideology of the newly founded Joseon. Back then, the publication of Confucian books was an urgent national task to promote the new dominant ideology. Most of all, the new dynasty needed technology to accurately print many books on neo-Confucianism, the new study introduced from China, without misspellings and left-out characters in a small volume and reprint them whenever necessary. It was metal movable typography that played this role. Accordingly, printing using movable metal type was something connected to the spiritual value related the founding principle of the state and had nothing to do with commercialization through popularization. "Just as woodblock printing was actively supported by the kings of the Goryeo dynasty, it was also the kings of Joseon that drove metal movable typography forward. The printing technology was not developed by individual entrepreneurs' investments, nor the need of the intellectual class. Of course, there was no possibility for printing technicians to use the technology for profits. This was not only true for the Goryeo dynasty and the early period of the Joseon dynasty but for the entire traditional societies

afterward. The technology could never be used to make money[28]."
In other words, movable metal type printing was never considered a
means for profit in Korea, unlike Europe. It was managed and pur-
sued thoroughly by the state as it was considered a national affair.
Taejong Sillok (The Annals of King Taejong) stated that "Students of
Confucianism could not read much because of a small number of
books available in Korea and it was hard to bring books from China
since it was located across the sea. At the same time, woodblocks engraved with characters could not print all the books in the world as
they were easily twisted and broken. That is why it was decided to
make bronze metal type to print and spread books[29]." The will of
King Taejong was clearly recorded. Neo-Confucianism was a new
study back then, and the number and kinds of neo-Confucian books
in Korea were limited. After the state's ideology was changed from
Buddhism to neo-Confucianism, it was necessary to print many
kinds of neo-Confucian books in a short period of time and keep a
few copies of each type in Korea in order to firmly establish the basis
for the nation. With the existing woodblock printing, however, it was
difficult to print all the books that Korea did not have among the
many neo-Confucian books in China and spread them in a short
time, nor was it possible to carve woodblocks to print numerous

28) Choi Jung-woo "*Comparative Study on Sociocultural Backgrounds behind the Printing
    Technology in Korea and Germany*" International Symposium on the Printing History
    in the East and the West (1997)
29) "*Taejong sllok*" Vol. 5. February in the 3rd year of King Taejong

books that were being newly published in China. It was decided to take advantage of metal movable type, as it was easy to separate movable type pieces after printing one book and re-typeset for another book, in order to increase the kinds and number of books. This illustrated that the printing of books in Korea was controlled thoroughly by the state. Books printed in this process were not sold but distributed. Books belonged to the sacred and spiritual domain in Korea. This made it impossible for books to be goods for transactions. It was much later that books started to be traded privately, and it was only after the 1870s that books were commercialized in earnest after printing technology from the West was reintroduced through Japan[30]. This was the fundamental reason why the history of printing technology unfolded in obviously different directions in Asia and Europe.

Attempts were made to find reasons why Korea's metal movable printing fail to bring mass duplication and the exponential expansion of knowledge as it did in Europe and why it coexisted with woodblock printing during the whole period of Joseon in the technical and phys-

---

30) It was 1883 when "Hanseong sunbo, the first Korean newspaper was printed. Park, Young-hyo is known to bring Japanese reporters and printing technicians from Japan to assist newspaper production. Before that, Japanese living in Busan was publishing "Joseon sinbo," a newspaper in Japanese language, and it is assumed that they would have printing equipment including movable metal type pieces in 1879 to print the newspaper. Jung Jin-seok *The Creation of Media and Publication Culture during the Time of Enlightenment*" The Oriental Studies 34th issue (2003), Institute of Oriental Studies, Dankook University. p,241

ical aspects of the typography. There were also valid deductions. Korea's movable metal type did not move away from the manual printing method as it remained at the level achieved during the rule of King Sejong the Great[31]. Because of the characteristics of letters that adopted the gather write method, both the Korean alphabet and Chinese characters required a disproportionately large number of movable type pieces for printing, compared to Western alphabets[32]. There is one additional point to be mentioned: it was difficult for the private sector to use metal—a precious material under the control of the state—for casting movable type pieces. Therefore, woodblock printing would remain a general practice for books with constant demand, and it did not disappear, but coexisted with movable type printing during the whole Joseon period. Metal movable typography was not synonymous with "efficiency" or "mass production," the so-called virtues of the technology. Contrary to what have been stated, Korea invented the "world's first" metal movable type even though it did not pursue "efficiency" or "effectiveness," and the invention did

---

31) Gang, Myeong-gwan "The History of Books and Knowledge during Joseon Dynasty" Seoul: Imagination for a Thousand Years, 2014. p,111

32) Joseon cast over 100,000 movable metal type pieces from a single casting. For example, over 100,000 movable type pieces was cast for Gyemi type (the 3rd year of King Taejong, 1403); 200,000 for Gapin type (the 16th year of King Sejong, 1434), and 300,000 for Gapjin type (the 15th year of King Seongjong in 1484). It was such an enormous amount. In Europe, on the other hand, the number of alphabets needed for printing a book was extremely limited. The 42-line Bible, for example, was printed with 292 movable metal type pieces. Füssel, Stephan: *Gutenberg und seine Wirkung.* Frankfurt am Main u. Leipzig : Insel, 1999, p. 15.

not die out on the grounds of being unfit for mass duplication while making a splendid culture of movable type flourish. Maybe it was because the movable metal type sufficiently fulfilled its own role expected by the society.

In Korea, during the Joseon period, in which woodblock printing was fulfilling the purpose of printing, mass duplication and popular dissemination of knowledge, "metal movable typography was developed for small-scale printing while competing against woodblock printed books. This helped movable metal type printing technology be improved to save manpower, resources, and storage space and print authoritative books in small quantities rather than improve economic feasibility and printing speed[33]." In this context, it could be understood why movable type print *"Goryeosa"* (History of Goryeo)[34] or *"Joseon Wangjo Sillok"* (The Annals of the Joseon Dynasty), which were listed in UNESCO's Memory of the World registry, were put in repositories instead of being widely distributed[35]. The neo-Confucian books, which had constant and huge demand, used to be republished

33) Nam, Young *"Reconsideration on the History before and after the Development of the Movable Metal Type Printing—from "Superiority or Inferiority of the Technology to Cultural Diversity"* "Journal of Chung-Ang Historical Studies" 29th issue (2009), p.28
34) The history book of Goryeo, of which compilation was started in 1449 (the 31st year of King Sejong) and completed in 1451 (the 1st year of King Munjong), consist of 139 volumes in total.
35) Seol, Seok-gyu "The Background and Its Meaning of Carving Confucianism on Woodblocks during the Joseon Dynasty" Korean Studies, 6th issue (2005) p.101

by woodblock printing for mass production based on the original books printed by movable metal type that were sent from the capital.

What kind of books did the Joseon dynasty print by movable type? In addition to the already mentioned "*Joseon Wangjo Sillok*" and "*Goryeosa,*" there are a number of books of importance: "*Sibchil sacheon gogeum tongyo*" (十七史纂古今通要), a Chinese history book that was compiled by Ho, Jeongbang of Yuan is worth citing because it was printed with the *Gyemija* type casted in the third year of King *Tae-jong* (1403); and "*Jachi tonggam gangmok*" (資治通鑑綱目), and "*Sagi*" (史記, Historical Record) and other Chinese history books are cases in point for books printed using the *Gyeongaja* type in the second year of King *Sejong* (1420). There are also books printed with the *Gabinja* type in the sixteenth year of King Sejong (1434): *Daehak yeonui* (大學衍義) and "*Chunchu Gyeongjeon Jibhae*" (春秋經傳集解), "*Geunsarok*" (近思錄) and the guide and introductory books for Confucian books and *Bunryu boju Leetaebaek si* (分類補註李太白詩), a book for literature. In the 29th year of King Sejong (1447), the first movable type in Korean was made to print "*Wolincheongangjigok*" (月印千江之曲) and "*Seokbo Sangjeol*" (釋譜詳節). There are also books printed using the *Eulhaeja* type casted in the first year of King Sejo (1455): "*Geumgang banyabaramil gyeong*" (金剛般若波羅密經) and other Buddhist scriptures reflecting the King's personal preference: "*Dongmunseon*" (東文選, Anthology of Korean Literature) and other anthologies; "*Dongguk*

Yeoji Seungnam" (東國輿地勝覽, the Survey of the Geography of Korea) and other geography books; as well as other basic books to help the intellectual class improve their refinement and strengthen the foundation of the state including "*Naehun*" (內訓, Instructions for Women). There are also books printed using the *Gapjinja* type casted in the 15th year of King Seongjong (1484): *Dongguk Tonggam* (東國通鑑, Comprehensive Mirror of The Eastern Kingdom) which compiled the history of the nation from the Ancient Joseon to the end of the Goryeo dynasty; "*Wang Hyeongmungong si*" (王荊文公詩, a collection of Wang, Ansung's poetic works) and "*Chanju byun-ryu dusi* (纂註分類杜詩, a collection of Dubo's poetic works)" and other anthologies. In addition to these, Joseon governments constantly used movable metal type to print books to help with the acquisition of and accurate understanding of neo-Confucianism, such as "*Daehak eonhae*" (大學諺

Wolincheongangjigok (1448), the first book printed by movable metal type in Korean

解, Annotation to Great Learning in Hangul), "*Maengja eonhae*" (孟子諺解, Annotation to Mencius in Hangul), and "*Sohak eonhae*" (小學諺解, Annotation to Basic Learning in Hangul)[36].

36) Cheon Hye-bong "*History of Korea's Movable Metal Printing*" Seoul: Bumwoo, 2012. p. 449-453 "The Chronological Table of Korean Movable Metal Types"

The importance of the movable metal printing in Korea should be understood in the context of accurate records, education, and delivery to future generations rather than of a mass dissemination of knowledge because the invention of metal movable type itself was not for mass duplication but for printing correct and authoritative books beyond the limitations of transcription and woodblock printing. At that time, woodblock printing alone could meet the demand for books in the Korean society, thus in Korea, the role of movable metal printing (mass production) was not as important and urgent as it was in Europe. Since the role of metal movable type was to print and store valuable books in small quantities, instead of mass production, in Koreans' imagination, books printed by metal movable type were not duplications but something with "auras of authenticity and a unique presence[37]."

---

37) Benjamin, Walter. "Das Kunstwerk im Zeitalter seiner technischen Reproduzierbarkeit" (erste deutsche Fassung, 1935), in: *Gesammelte Schriften. Band I, Werkausgabe Band 2,* hrsg. v. R. Tiedemann/H. Schweppenhäuser. Suhrkamp : Frankfurt am Main 1980, p. 431–469.

IV

Social Transformation
through Printing Technology

1. The Reformation

When the first printing press appeared, the Catholic Church believed the new technology was a present from God. The Crusaders assembled to overthrow Turkey started the "first religious movement" by printing indulgences in large quantities to raise money for the war. It was, however, the reformation movement led by Martin Luther that first realized the function of printing technology for mass media, in particular, as a reformist force not for the ruling Catholic Church but for the transformation of the existing society. Since his *Ninety-five Theses of 1517* to the Roman Catholic Church, some 7,900 of Luther's books were published by the end of the 16th century[38]. This was the evidence that clearly shows the relationship between printing tech-

---

38) Fuchs, Thomas. "Buch und Revolution", in: *Buch und Revolution. Beiträge zur Buch- und Bibliotheksgeschichte Mitteldeutschlands im 16. Jahrhundert*, hrsg. v. E. Bünz/T. Fuchs/S. Rhein. Leipzig, 2015, pp. 9-38, p. 25. According to USTC (Universal Short Title Catalogue), a collective database of all books published in Europe between the invention of printing and the end of the sixteenth century, the number of printed books which were classified as Luther's books between 1511 and 1600 reached 7,750.

nology and the Reformation.

An indulgence printed by Gutenberg in 1454 and housed in the Herzog August Library

The Reformation in Europe was the first mass movement that utilized printing technology for anti-regime propaganda or demagogy. An enormous number of pamphlets were printed in mother languages instead of Latin to gain support from the general public and early religious reformers, including Martin Luther, Philipp Melanchthon, and Ulrich Zwingli became revolutionists with the help of the technology without realizing it themselves.

"How many presses there be in the world, so many block-houses there be against the high castle of St. Angelo, so that either the Pope must abolish knowledge and printing, or printing at length will root him out[39]."

Was the religious situation in the early 16th century unstable enough

---

39) Eisenstein, Elizabeth. *The Printing Revolution in Early Modern Europe*, Cambridge University Press, 1983, p. 132.

to inevitably cause religious reform or revolutionary confusion? Did Europe at that time really desire the emergence of Luther? The historical facts known so far suggest that European society in the early 16th century was far more stable than what is generally believed. Although European society and the church system were relatively stabilized around 1500AD, 50 years after the invention of Gutenberg's printing, the political consciousness of the general public was greatly changed. In particular, the laity came to have a dramatically changed perception of the Bible, the exclusive property of the Catholic Church. In the past, bibles in mother tongues had been holy books that the common people could neither possess nor read personally. After the invention of printing, however, bibles were widely spread through printing. In particular, the spread of bibles in mother languages that the common people could read came to threaten the exclusive right of the Catholic Church to the holy book. In 1486, the Archbishop of Cologne prohibited the publication of bibles written in mother languages[40]. Before the Reformation was started by Luther, eighteen different German bibles were printed in Germany alone, and the number of issues exceeded 10,000[41]. The mass duplication and dissemination of bibles in mother tongues led to endless questions raised

---

40) Kapp, Friedrich: *Geschichte des Deutschen Buchhandels. Band 1: Geschichte des Deutschen Buchhandels bis in das siebzehnte Jahrhundert*, Verlag des Börsenvereins der Deutschen Buchhändler, Leipzig 1886 (Reprint), p. 529.

41) Choi, Kaung-eun *"From Transcription to Printing—Centered on the Bibles Printed in German before the Luther Bible"* Seoul: History of the Korean Culture, 2016.

to the traditional Catholic Church. By then, it was not possible for the Catholic Church to further delay conflicts surrounding the newly emerged issues about the privileges of the clergy and religious studies.

"A Sermon on Indulgences and Grace," printed version of Luther which triggered the Reformation (1518)

"Transcription by the laity and the development of a printing culture pulled down the ideological superiority of the Church. Commercial transcription workshops and the growth of printing companies following it made it difficult for the church authorities which previously directly controlled the means of book production to effectively censor[42]."

It could be inferred that even if Luther and other early religious reformers died before they had made their arguments, someone else, with the help of the new printing technology, could have achieved the purpose of the Gospel by elevating the education of the laity. The Reformation through Luther

---

42) Curran, J., Communication, Power and Social Order, In: M. Gurevitch/T. Bennett/J. Curran/J. Woolacott eds. *Culture, Society and Media*. London 1982, p. 218.

and the resulting religious civil wars such as the Thirty Years' War might have been avoided. Even so, a second Luther would have appeared somewhere in Europe to start a religious reform due to the influence of printing. In conclusion, the invention and the proliferation of printing in the 15th century acted as the most crucial driver to bring down the relatively stable European society and the Catholic Church in the 16th century to establish a new social order.

2. The Maintenance of Order and the Stabilization of System

As discussed in Chapter 3, the metal movable type in Korea had purposes and functions totally different from those of Europe. Nevertheless, it is true that Korea's metal movable typography has been underestimated for its social role compared to Gutenberg's aggressive and dynamic force for commercialization and the popularization of knowledge and information as well as the resulting revolutionary changes in society. It is well known that printing played the role of both a means of mass reproduction and a stimulus for the popularization of knowledge in Europe. In such analyses, an error of orientalism-based interpretation, efforts to find the value and importance of Korea's movable metal printing from the European perspective, could be found.

Even the analysis by European scholars[43], who have served as the criteria for such assessment, often reveal such error because they were not based on the in-depth understanding of the Korean situation back then, and even lead to the conclusion that Korea's typography had had only "minimum" socio-cultural impact. Even after accepting such European points of view toward printing technology, there are still facts that have been overlooked by Western scholars.

First of all, concerning the metal movable typography and the use of mother language, Korea's unique situation—the intervention of *Hangul* (the Korean alphabet) was ignored. The official name of Hangul when it was invented was *Hunminjeongeum* meaning Proper Sounds for the Instruction of the People. The motive for the creation was clearly stated in the first part, King Sejong's preface of "*Hunmin-jeongeum Haeryebon*" (the printed edition of Explanations and Examples of the Correct/ Proper Sounds for the Instruction of the People) published in the 28th year of King Sejong (1446). In the preface, the king articulated that he created the Korean alphabet "to help all the Korean people easily learn 28 letters that he created after he felt the need for new letters different from the Chinese characters to help his people to express their opinions[44]." In other words, *Hangul*

---

43) Case in point, Volti, Rudi, *Society and Technological Change*, New York, Worth Publishers, 2001, p. 187.

44) The newly created Hangul was used for the purpose of maintaining the order of the State, such as for translation for Buddhist and Confucian scriptures. The creation of Hangul by King Sejong was not the product of the so-called "humanism"-based

was invented as an auxiliary means for strengthening the rule of the state to establish an ideal state based on the neo-Confucian ideology, and to this end, the creation was intended to spread and deliver information on the neo-Confucian ideology.

Despite the king's wishes, *Hangul* was "used limitedly by central government officials and for gentry literature or letters written by women[45]" in its early days, and it took over a century after its creation to be widely used by ordinary Koreans[46]. "It is suitable to say that the reading public started to be formed in earnest in the 18th century or in the later part of the 18th century, when printed books were published and professional writers who made their livings from their creations appeared[47]." *Hangul* was not letters that had passed down from a long time ago, instead it underwent the process of "creation," "proclamation," and "dissemination." That is why it took over 300 years until "far-reaching classes of readers who could read and write *Hangul*" were formed and mass consumption of Korean printings

modern spirit. It was created "by the need of the royal family, not driven by the demand from people. Some viewed Hangul as the trophy that Korean people earned as their power grew, but the view was a result obtained by interpreting the historical context in which Hangul realized its popular values, and does not explain the true intention of the creation." Choi Kyeong-bong "*Hangul Democracy*" With Books: 2012, p.25

45) Song, Ho-geun "*The Birth of the People*" Seoul: Minumsa, 2011. p.179
46) Ahn, Byeong-hee "*The Study of Hunminjeongeum*" Seoul: Seoul National University Press, 2007. pp. 245-252.
47) Song, Ho-geun "*The Birth of the People*" Seoul: Minumsa, 2011. p.290

happened. After the 18ᵗʰ century, however, *Hangul* firmly became the letters of the ordinary people and played a central role in their letter usages. Metal movable printing went through a slow and gradual process to raise awareness of general people through *Hangul*, which allowed the technology to function as a driver for gradual social transformations instead of the revolutionary social reform in Europe.

Unlike in Europe, Korea's metal movable printing did not become the driving force for social transformation like the Reformation. As in Europe, the first printings using the early metal movable type were religious scriptures. Buddhist scriptures including the *Jikji* were religious books in nature, and although there might be controversy over whether or not neo-Confucianism had the status of a religion in Joseon, it is true that it was the ruling principle of the state and the ruling ideology of the society.

During the early Joseon dynasty, for example, when movable metal printing technology peaked in Korea, neo-Confucianism was the secular ideology for the ruling class. Of course kings existed, but Joseon by its nature was the state of the gentry, the intellectual class. Intellectual individuals were directly involved in ruling after they passed the state-administered examination, and were potential candidates for the ruling class even if they were not in official posts. Confucian books, such as the Analects of Confucius and Mencius were textbooks to prepare for the state examination, and represented the only opportunity to become state officials in a fair way. This shows a direct relationship between printing technology and the neo-Confucianism education of the gentry, which was essential for maintaining the social system. Such a ruling organization consisting of the intellectual class was strong enough not to be disrupted by the internal friction. This could be proven by the fact that Joseon's governance of rule by the intellectual class, who were educated with neo-Confucian ideas, was kept to the end of the 19th century without losing its firm base. Intellectuals with the will for social reform, including scholars of the Realist School of Confucianism, also wanted reform within the framework of neo-Confucianism. For Joseon, which took pride in being the legitimate successor of the ideology after the fall of the Ming dynasty, neo-Confucianism was not something to reform. In short, the mass proliferation of books containing the innovative thinking of intellectuals following the development of printing never threatened the status of the state ideology.

The reform of neo-Confucianism in Korea was not done from the inside by the intellectual class who knew the ideology well. As a result, it was attacked, rejected, and supplemented by other ideologies. The state ideology, which sustained the Joseon dynasty for some 500 years, was criticized and denied by the *Donghak* (an academic movement in Korean neo-Confucianism), a naturally grown religion and grassroots movement started in the 1860s, and Roman Catholicism, which was introduced from the West and accepted after countless martyrs died in the 19th century. It became the reason why Korea's neo-Confucianism rapidly became nominal in the 20th century and afterward, instead of undergoing fiercely internal criticism and reform to persistently survive in society. Since then, the tradition and custom of Korea's neo-Confucianism were changed and reduced. It can be concluded that printing technology in Korea was not a means to reform the religion and the dominant ideology of the state. On the contrary, it played a social role opposite from the West as it was used to enhance and systematize the ideology to lay the foundation for the establishment of a "deep-rooted" unshakable nation.

It should be pointed out that in Korea, commerce had been suppressed as a subject of vigilance that could shake the foundation of agriculture, the key industry of the state, and collapse the agricultural community. This was because the disruption of rural communities would shake the order of social classes and the emergence of the wealthy merchant class through the accumulation of goods also would be a potential threat to the state since it could change the fundamental supporting principles of the Joseon society. In the Joseon society, in which the moral politics by poor but honest Confucian scholars was the ideal, the pursuit of profits through commerce was disparaged as tricks and artifice and markets took on negative meanings as they were described as places of corruption, irregularities, and lies. Thus, the development of the "market" for the mass production and sale of books was impeded.

This made social reform resulting from the creation of *Hangul* and the growth of popular printings for the general public undergo a much more gradual process in Korea than in Europe, which had completely different conditions. Like other human technological inventions, whether or not the technology itself was able to act as a driver for social reform in a short period of time depends on whether the innovative force of the technology in question had an environment suitable for the social conditions. What the Korean society wanted from the metal movable typography at the time of its invention was not the mass reproduction of information and, as a result, it did not lead to rapid and revolutionary social changes through the popularization of information. Therefore, Korea could be an example which proves the existence of a society in which the biggest function and role of the movable metal printing technology were not the mass reproduction of information. This also shows that Korea's movable metal printing sufficiently fulfilled the role that the society of the time required from it, the preservation of accurate knowledge based on printed books of authority.

V

Conclusion

It has been widely accepted that printing technology brought about revolution in human civilization, especially communication. Many well-known academic books including "*The Gutenberg Galaxy*" by Marshall McLuhan, "*The Printing Revolution in Early Modern Europe*" by Elizabeth L. Eisenstein, "*Communication and World Order Transformation*" by Ronald Deibert, and "*Printing in the Early Modern Era*" by Michael Giesecke described almost in unison how much Gutenberg's printing contributed to the development of civilization. As illustrated in the introduction, some even say that typography is the best invention of humankind in the last 1000 years. The invention of printing was thought to have put an end to the Middle Ages and bring about the Modern Era and was cited as one of the three best inventions for the development of civilization, along with gunpowder and the compass. These arguments, however, do not fully concur with the perspective of Asia, including Korea, which possesses the oldest extant movable metal type print book.

A glance into the duplication methods used in Asia and Europe before the invention of printing clearly reveals the differences between the two cultures. Europe used transcription for duplication. For about 100 years before Gutenberg, the so-called heyday of the transcription culture, transcription was the only replication method used in Europe and trade of manual transcriptions thrived all across Europe. Contrary to this, in Asia, woodblock printing was the method in the mainstream.

Against this backdrop, when looking more closely into the background of Gutenberg's printing and Korea's movable metal type, the unilateral argument that printing technology was the direct cause of the development of civilization starts to lose its credibility. The socio-cultural background for Gutenberg's printing in Europe was the Pan-European reading classes formed thanks to the full-blown transcription culture and the influence of the resulting capitalist market economy, while that of Korea's metal movable type was the desire for technical advancement following woodblock printing and the enhancement of the state's dominant ideology.

Like the phrase, "No reformation without book prinitng," printing had a tremendous impact on Western society. In Europe in the Middle Ages, which was united under the religion of Christianity, the church exercised unchallenged power. Christianity was the religion that upheld the Holy Book and the messengers of the Bible were churches and monasteries. The latter, in particular, were the only window that produced and supplied books including the bibles. The invention of printing, however, threatened the church's exclusive right to knowledge of letters. The laity's thirst for knowledge was satisfied with massive supply of printed books and the church relinquished its exclusive right to knowledge due to the usage of letters by the mundane world. Printing in Western society consequently emerged as a driving force for reform that broke down the existing society and played a decisive role in changing the time from the Middle Ages to the Modern Era.

The development course of printing in Asia, on the other hand, was different from that of Europe. Unlike in Europe, woodblock printing already existed in Korea before movable metal type. In this context, the invention of movable metal type could be understood as extended efforts to improve and further develop woodblock printing. Moreover, the socio-cultural background of Korea's movable metal type was to keep the order and stabilize the regime rather than social reform. Of course, such developments in Korea did not act as a driver for the sweeping social reforms that Europe saw. From a long-term perspective, however, it had a gradual but obvious impact on the spread of knowledge and the delivery of information, and in the end, laid the foundation for modern-day Korea to become an IT powerhouse.

aber steht der Stifter". *Ornamenta ecclesiae* (1985). pp. 117-148.

Curran, J. "Communication, Power and Social Order", in M. Gure-vitch/T. Bennett/J. Curran/J. Woolacott ed. *Culture, Society and Media*. London, 1982.

Deibert, Ronald. *Parchment, Printing, and Hypermedia. Communication in World Order Transformation*. Columbia University Press, 1997.

Eisenstein, Elizabeth. *The Printing Revolution in Early Modern Europe*, Cambridge University Press, 1983.

Febvre, Lucien/Henri Martin. *L'apparition du Livre*. Paris: Albin Michel, 1958.

Fuchs, Thomas. "Buch und Revolution", in: *Buch und Revolution. Beiträge zur Buch- und Bibliotheksgeschichte Mitteldeutschlands im 16. Jahrhundert*, hrsg. v. E. Bünz/T. Fuchs/S. Rhein. Leipzig, 2015, pp. 9-38.

Füssel, Stephan. *Gutenberg und Seine Wirkung*. Frankfurt am Main: Insel, 1999.

Füssel, Stephan. *Kommentar zu Leben und Werk von Johannes Gutenberg, zum Bibeldruck, den Besonderheiten des Göttinger Exemplars, dem "Göttinger Musterbuch" und dem "Helmaspergerschen Notariatsinstrument"*. Köln: Taschen, 2018.

Giesecke, Michael. *Der Buchdruck in der frühen Neuzeit*. Frankfurt am Main: Suhrkamp, 1994.

Kapp, Friedrich. *Geschichte des Deutschen Buchhandels. Band 1: Geschichte des Deutschen Buchhandels bis in das siebzehnte Jahrhundert*, Verlag des Börsenvereins der Deutschen Buchhändler, Leipzig, 1886. (Reprint).

McLuhan, Marshall. *The Gutenberg Galaxy. The making of typographic man*, University of Toronto Press, 1962.

Schmidt-Künsemüller, Fr. A. "Gutenbergs Schritt in die Technik". In: H. Widmann(Hg.), *Der gegenwärtige Stand der Gutenberg-Forschung* (1972), pp. 122-147.

Volti, Rudi. *Society and Technological Change*. New York: Worth Publishers, 2001.

Wittmann, R. *Geschichte des Deutschen Buchhandels*. 3.Aufl., München, 2011.

"*Jikji*," UNESCO's Memory of the World Programme and Cheongju

KIM, Seung Hwan

Professor of Korean Education, Chungbuk National University

I

"Jikji" and Memory of the World

On September 3, 2001, a UNESCO Memory of the World Conference was held in Cheongju, Korea. In many ways, it was meaningful that a UNESCO meeting was held in Cheongju, located about 130 km away from Seoul, the capital of South Korea. Delegations from countries around the world gathered in the conference room at Cheongju Art Center. After three hours of discussion and deliberation, a decision was made to inscribe *"Jikji"* and 40 other cultural heritages on the Memory of the World Register. The final report of that day included an interesting fact: "Although the Republic of Korea submitted *"Buljo jikjisimcheyojeol"* (the second volume of "Anthology of Great Buddhist Priests' Zen Teachings or simply *"Jikji"*) as a Memory of the World, the actual document is possessed by the National Library of France." What makes the statement interesting is a very delicate logic behind it. It was indirectly saying that the submission for the inscription on the Memory of the World Register should be made by a state or an organization that owns the recorded document. Thus, it implied that the submission of *Jikji* by South Korea did not conform to the general rules of the Memory of the Safeguard World Programme, but the next sentence revealed how that issue was discussed. It stated, "It is suggested that Korea and France work together on the digitization project of this book to make it widely accessible, and have it translated to English and French with scholarly introductions[1]." This means that the owner of *Jikji* is France, but Korea also has responsibilities for and the right to *Jikji* since Korea produced the record. In other words, France, the owner, and Korea, the producer of *Jikji* have different authorities and both nations should work together to make this valuable cultural heritage better known to the world.

The 5th Meeting of the International Advisory Committee of the Memory of the World Programme

---

1) It is suggested that Korea and France work together on the digitization project of this book to make it widely accessible, and have it translated to English and French with scholarly introductions. FINAL REPORT, Memory of the World Programme, UNESCO, Paris, August, 2001.

II

The Value and Meaning of the Inscription on the Memory of the World

1. The Meaning of the Memory of the World

To explain about the Memory of the World, it is necessary to know about UNESCO, the organization that established and operates the program because the Memory of the World is one of UNESCO's important programs. UNESCO establishes a variety of subordinate organizations depending on the purpose and intention of their establishment to operate a variety of programs. Such organizations and programs have contributed to the development of culture and the education of science of humanity. UNESCO has become the world's largest organization because its spirit and purpose is needed and respectable. Therefore, it is necessary to examine what cultural and historical values "*Jikji*" has in the spirit of UNESCO and what significance that the values may have for people across the world. What does UNESCO do?

UNESCO was established in 1945 with the following purpose: The purpose of the Organization is to contribute to peace and security by promoting collaboration among nations through education, science, and culture in order to further universal respect for justice, for the rule of law, and for the human rights and fundamental freedoms which are affirmed for the peoples of the world, without distinction of race, sex, language, or religion, by the Charter of the United Nations[2]." Its official name is United Nations Educational Scientific and Cultural Organization (UNESCO). It was established based on deep regret of the First and Second World Wars. Mass casualties and destruction from the two rounds of world wars meant humanity had to find a new path, then, around 1943, when the Allied Forces were expected to win, preparations were made to establish the United Nations (UN) and UNESCO for the areas of education, science, and culture. On October 24, 1945, the UN was launched for World Peace. UNESCO is a UN affiliate handling the politics, diplomacy, peace, economy, and industry and realizing the UN's objectives in the areas of education, science, and culture.

Against this historical background, in November 1945, delegations from 44 nations gathered in London, UK to hold the international

---

2) UNESCO, Constitution. Article I Purposes and functions. The purpose of the Organization is to contribute to peace and security by promoting collaboration among the nations through education, science and culture in order to further universal respect for justice, for the rule of law and for the human rights and fundamental freedoms which are affirmed for the peoples of the world, without distinction of race, sex, language or religion, by the Charter of the United Nations.

conference to launch UNESCO. At this gathering, Ellen Wilkinson, the then education minister of the UK, declared equal opportunity for education, the objective realization of common values, the free exchange of knowledge and ideas, and mutual understanding and cooperation. The first General Conference of UNESCO was held in Paris, France from November 19 to December 10, 1946. At the conference, Julian Huxley from the UK, who contributed to the popularization of science, was elected as the first Director General of UNESCO. The UN affiliate is headquartered in Paris, France, and is the world's largest international body with 195 member states and ten associate members with 55 regional offices and eleven directly-run research institutes. Its Director General, who serves a six-year term, plays a substantial role beyond the symbolic role of a representative, and the General Conference which is held every two years is the top decision making body. The Secretariat conducts the basic work of UNESCO and executes decisions made at the General Conference, and for its execution, the Executive Body was formed with a four-year term. National commissions for UNESCO are established in all member states to handle various duties.

UNESCO could have become a large and important organization because it is operated in a democratic and open manner under the ultimate goal of sustainable development based on peace and prosperity. However, it has faced criticism since its operation is centered on the West and economic powerhouses while it is sometimes used as a means for politics and diplomacy. Its fundamental purpose is peace and cooperation. In particular, it endeavors to support science and technology research, promote art and culture, and create a peaceful and prosperous world through education that develops the minds of people. That is why it takes the eradication of illiteracy and general education seriously. In particular, it recommends and assists each nation, people, region, and religion to maintain their cultural uniqueness under the motto of multiculturalism and cultural diversity. In this regard, the Convention on the Safeguarding of the Diversity of Cultural Contents, discussed in 2001, is an important document which symbolizes the spirit of UNESCO. The principle of multiculturalism and the basis for cultural diversity are being realized through the preservation of the world's cultural heritages.

In order to realize biological diversity and cultural diversity, UNESCO, since 1972, has designated cultural and natural heritages, and mixed heritages (for example, Machu Picchu in Peru) to preserve and safeguard them. Biological diversity is to safeguard and conserve nature and diverse ecosystems while cultural diversity is to safeguard and preserve various aspects of history and culture. In particular, UNESCO recommends the designation of world heritage sites and intangible cultural heritages to safeguard and utilize them. Among the many committees of the body, the UNESCO Memory of the

World Programme for documentary heritages draws particular interest. The criteria for the safeguarding and conservation of cultural heritages and properties are universality, meaning, value, and time. UNESCO pursues the universal values of humanity, moving beyond discrimination on the grounds of region, religion, gender, economy, politics, and educational attainment, while making efforts to respect the authenticity of the respective people and nations.

2. The Conservation and Utilization of Cultural Heritages and Properties

The Logo of World Heritage

In 2001, *Jikji* was inscribed on the Memory of the World Register, another program separate from the World Heritage. Since there are a number of culture-related organizations and programs, they might be needed to be explained here. The first convention on cultural heritage was "The Convention Concerning the Protection of the World Cultural and Natural Heritage" concluded in November 1972. According to the convention, it was decided at the 17th session of the General Conference to Designate UNESCO World Heritage Sites, which protects and utilizes cultural heritages in most nations. Along with the agreement to preserve and utilize the Memory of the World Programme from 1996, many bylaws on cultural heritages have been used for operation and implementation. Nonetheless, since UNESCO uses a few concepts including world heritage, documentary heritage, cultural heritage, etc. in a mixed manner, it may sometimes cause confusion. Then, what is the accurate concept of cultural heritage? First, a cultural heritage is a tangible or intangible product with cultural value and is the concept that emphasizes the legacy of the past. It should be understood in the temporal context that connects the past, the present, and the future, and aims to well preserve and utilize heritage inherited from ancestors and pass them down to future generations. Second, cultural properties are the tangible or intangible product with cultural value and are the concept which emphasizes that culture is also goods. Goods are materials that have economic value and satisfy human desires. This means that the word "cultural property" considers culture as the economic concept of capitalism. Third, a cultural asset is the concept that highlights the concrete reality of value, such as goods and rights. Unlike cultural properties, a cultural asset implies that the possessed value has the possibility for development in the future. Fourth, a culture capital, coined by a sociologist Pierre Bourdieu, is a concept in contrast to economic capital. He classified it into three categories: objectified cultural capital that can be possessed like paintings and drawings; embodied cultural capital that can be materialized, including the capability to enjoy music; and institutional cultural capital that has been institutionalized, such as a sommelier certificate. Cultural property and assets have the characteristics of cultural capital. However, since cultural property is a sociological concept, it would be appropriate to use depending on the context. Among the above mentioned concepts, the most universally used concept is cultural heritage.

Cultural heritage is a concept that syntactically connects the past, the present and the future and emphasizes the responsibilities and obligations of the current generation. Depending on the form of cultural heritage, it can be divided into two parts: tangible culture, such as structures, monuments, natural landscapes, books, art pieces, and sculptures; and intangible culture, including languages, traditions, folksongs, knowledge, and the form of art. However, when actually classifying cultural heritage, it can be divided into three parts. The first is cultural property, which is culture with a physical presence such as buildings and other unmovable objects, and movable ones such as books. Cultural property, in general, refers to tangible heritage. The second is intangible culture, which is related to human activities like customs, beliefs, ways to create art, and ideas. Although they do not have a form, they are worth preserving and utilizing. The third is natural heritage, which is plants, animals, natural environments, and natural landscapes. However, this concept is slightly different from cultural heritage in that nature is not culture that is created and accumulated by humans.

The concept of cultural heritage was changed to a large extent in the 21st century. It was first argued that since preserving cultural heritage from the past as it was would be considered taxidermied preservation, and this should be actively utilized. This means that while it is necessary to exhibit these items in museums and keep them in repositories, they should be endowed with present values, while contributing to production and development. After such arguments were made, preservation methods were drastically advanced with computers and digital technology in the 21st century. This is useful for the culture industry as well, so every nation is endeavoring to develop its cultural property industry. According to such changes in the cultural environment, UNESCO is seeking ways to preserve and utilize cultural heritages, and pass them down to future generations from various perspectives. For their part, all the nations and peoples are discussing the conservation of culture from diverse angles and implementing them faithfully. The same goes for many local areas in each nation, and preservation and the utilization of culture is being carried out at the world, national and local levels. In this context, layers of culture can be divided into three parts: world culture, national culture, and local culture, but the multi-layered division makes effective management and conservation difficult.

The vision and responsibility of the Memory of the World Programme, which UNESCO operates to turn local and national culture into world culture, is as follows:

2.3.1 Accordingly, the vision of the Memory of the World Programme is that the world's documentary heritage belongs to all, should be fully preserved and protected for all and, with due recognition of cultural mores and practicalities, should be permanently accessible to all without hindrance.

2.3.2 The mission of the Memory of the World Programme is to increase awareness and protection of the world's documentary heritage, and achieve its universal and permanent accessibility[3].

This means that global awareness of the existence and importance of documentary heritage should be increased, that best technological practices should help the preservation of the world's documentary

---

3) 2.3.1 Accordingly, the vision of the Memory of the World Programme is that the world"s documentary heritage belongs to all, should be fully preserved and protected for all and, with due recognition of cultural mores and practicalities, should be permanently accessible to all without hindrance.
2.3.2 The mission of the Memory of the World Programme is to increase awareness and protection of the world"s documentary heritage, and achieve its universal and permanent accessibility.
http://unesdoc.unesco.org/images/0012/001256/125637e.pdf access Sep., 15, 2018.
GENERAL GUIDELINES TO SAFEGUARD DOCUMENTARY HERITAGE. CII-95/WS-11rev February 2002

heritage, and that they should be easily and rapidly accessed and utilized by all people. This talks about the preservation of cultural diversity and the protection and utilization of cultural heritages among the many purposes of UNESCO's establishment. At the same time, it is to create cultural value that can be shared by people across the

The logo of the Memory of the World Programme

world. Among all the various cultural programs and organizations, it is the UNESCO Memory of the World Programme that is related to "*Jikji,*" the cultural heritage. Then, what process do cultural heritages such as *Jikji* undergo for inscription?

3. The Inscription Process of the Memory of the World

The criteria for a cultural heritage may differ depending on the nation and its people. The Memory of the World puts stress on universality and generality to leave cultural heritages that can be shared by all of the people across the world and shall be remembered and passed down to future generations. That is why the protection and preservation of cultural assets and property are decided based on universality, meaning, value, and time. The criteria set by the Memory of the World Committee are as follows: 1) the influence of the documentary heritage in question on world history; 2) a time that reflects an important period of the history or a specific change; 3) a place which may contain crucial information about a locality and location; 4) people who contributed to history and culture; 5) an important subject or theme; 6) a form and style that can be an important sample; or 7) social, cultural, and spiritual value. The following is the documented criteria for the inscription on the Memory of the World Register[4].

The 3rd Meeting of the International Advisory Committee of Memory of the World Programme

---

4) Textual items such as manuscripts, books, newspapers, posters, etc. The textual content may be recorded in ink, pencil, paint or other medium.
   The carrier may be of paper, plastic, papyrus, parchment, palm leaves, bark, textile fabric, stone or other medium.
   Similarly, non-textual items such as drawings, prints, maps, music.
   Audiovisual items such as films, discs, tapes and photographs - whether recorded in analogue or digital formats, and by mechanical, electronic or other means.

① Textual items such as manuscripts, books, newspapers, posters, etc. The carrier may be of paper, plastic, papyrus, parchment, palm leaves, bark, textile fabric, stone, or other medium.

② Non-textual items such as drawings, prints, maps, or music

③ Traditional movements and the video images related to them

④ Audiovisual items such as films, discs, tapes, and photographs - whether recorded in analogue or digital formats, and by mechanical, electronic, or other means

The criteria encompass all documentary heritages including documents and non-documentary heritages such as drawings, music, images, and digital materials. This shows that the Memory of the World Programme is a recollection program to "remember." Remembering something means that it is something important and should be passed down to future generations. Yet, the value of the document itself is more important than the inscription criteria of the World Record Heritage Register or subjects to be inscribed. This means what is recorded is important, but other things are more important: the method of how they were documented, the overall state, the state that shows how well they are preserved, and the technical aspects of documents. The Bible and Buddhist scriptures, for example, are not the Memory of the World. Although they are old and have value, they do not have documentary and cultural value. From this point of view, "*Jikji*" was inscribed on the Register because it was recognized for its value, time, place, style, and form as a book printed by movable metal type. The inscription process is as follows:

① The registration application to be submitted by individuals, associations, and organizations to the UNESCO Programme of General Information

② Deliberation by the UNESCO subcommittees

③ UNESCO subcommittees' submission of their review and recommendation to the International Advisory Committee (IAC)

④ Final review and registration recommendation by the IAC

⑤ Approval by the UNESCO Director General

The inscription to the Register means remembering the history of mankind. Humanity always exists through memory and records. Modern human beings appeared around 200,000 years ago, the first civilization appeared about 12,000 years ago, and people started to leave history and records from about 5,000 years ago. The Memory of the World Programme is the program related to cultural heritage during the time of history after prehistoric times. The ultimate goal of the program is to remember record-related cultural heritage among the remains and relics of the Age of History. If the humanity of the present leaves valuable assets through records to the future generations, they will do so for generations to come after them. Since it is wise to both safeguard these assets and preserve them to pass down later, UNESCO is making efforts to make a variety of culture be utilized and preserved. This is why it started to increase accessibility, or in other words, usability, when inscribing *Jikji* to the Register.

4. The Spirit of Cultural Diversity

When it was decided that *Jikji* was to be listed on the Memory of the World Register, cultural diversity was given as the theoretical grounds for the decision. As mentioned above, the program is in operation to safeguard and utilize the diverse culture of various peoples and nations. This is because if the diversity of culture is not well maintained, it can threaten the very survival of mankind. This leads to the next question: Why is it important to preserve cultural diversity? Cultural diversity is in the same context with the biological diversity that was adopted in Nairobi, Kenya, in 1992. In other words, cultural diversity is based on cultural democracy, which means mutual respect for cultural characteristics of all localities and people and the acceptance of cultural differences, in the spirit of multiculturalism. All people have the fundamental right to keep and enjoy their own culture. This means that cultural diversity is a theory and a policy that no one should be discriminated against on the grounds of nationality, people, region, race, religion, language, gender, generation, age, educational attainment, locality, or personal preference. In particular, it means respect for diverse cultural layers, mutual communication, and it is a policy for and discourse on the enhancement of the cultural rights of individuals and groups, and a global movement to safeguard different species of culture.

Cultural diversity was started with the objective to promote sustainable development through mutual understanding and cooperation while different cultures of diverse peoples and of regions peacefully coexist. In particular, the globalization driven by the two axes of growth development and science and technology not only exploits nature but threatens unique cultures. As the capitalist globalization advances, culture is likely to be standardized in the name of universal culture or global culture. In this context, discourse on cultural diversity has an implication of a time to avoid cultural conflicts and confrontations derived from the advancement of the globalization while maintaining a healthy cultural environment[5]. In this regard, multiculturalism, cultural diversity, cultural pluralism, cultural identities, cultural uniqueness, and cultural tradition are the basis of life that are the most important for and valuable to people.

UNESCO declared "UNESCO Universal Declaration on Cultural Diversity" at the 31st General Conference in 2001. The convention

---

5) UNESCO, UNIVERSAL DECLARATION ON CULTURAL DIVERSITY, 2001.

was cited at different levels in 2003, 2005, 2007, and 2009, and a number of nations rectified it or agreed on it. The declaration made it clear that culture is a fundamental human right while emphasizing i) that respective cultures have their own uniqueness and ii) that mutual recognition and intercultural dialogue for culture is needed. It also clearly stated that culture should be preserved and conserved as it is the institution of mankind that contains unique value for humankind. The spirit of cultural diversity is to safeguard the unique culture of each people and nation while respecting that of others. However, some argue that cultural uniformity or mono-culturalism, as opposed to cultural diversity and multiculturalism, should be kept.

Mono-culturalism and cultural uniformity—for example, a religion-centered belief that the world should be united by religion, ideological hegemony, or cultural nationalism—threatens the cultural ecosystem. Cultural diversity faces criticism in many ways. It is argued that in the era of globalization, culture also has no choice but to pursue the uniform standard, criteria, assessment, and form and style. Some also criticize cultural diversity as being a political and economic monopoly disguised as diversity and the argument for the cultural hegemony of the Western society. Others argue that cultural universalism can also acknowledge cultural distinctiveness, authenticity, and differentiation and that cultural uniformity is better. They were met with the counter-argument that culture is not a subject for trade, like industrial goods. All of these contradicting views are related to this question, "Can a general geo-culture, which can be shared by the entire human race, be created?" UNESCO believes that there should be a culture shared by all of humanity and there are such cultural heritages. They are the world heritages and the world documentary heritages.

5. The Value of *Jikji* as a World Documentary Heritage

The final report for *Jikji*'s inscription on the Memory of the World Register expressed the value that it had as movable metal type as follows: "The nomination is an important document: the earliest known example in the world of printing by the use of moveable metal type. It is a unique survivor from this early period, suggesting that moveable metal type, an invention of enormous global impact" was first developed in Korea[6]." It consists of three propositions: 1) movable metal type was an invention of enormous global impact; 2) movable metal type was invented in Korea; and 3) therefore, *Jikji* printed in Korea is important, and should be well preserved and widely known. Nonetheless, it did not state that the movable metal type invented in Korea significantly impacted the world. This implies

---

6) The nomination is an important document: the earliest known example in the world of printing by use of moveable metal types. It is a unique survivor from this early period, suggesting that moveable metal type. "an invention of enormous global impact" was first developed in Korea.

that the invention of movable metal type does not coincide with the influence of it. In other words, it was saying that "the movable metal type developed by Gutenberg from Germany had a great impact on the world, but it turned out that movable metal type was developed in Korea first.

Then, what is the position that Korea should take as the proud developer of movable metal type? Korea cannot argue that it invented movable metal type and the type that it invented had a huge impact on the cultural history of the world because, as mentioned above, the development of movable metal type does not coincide with the influence of it. In addition, as many nations including China, Japan, Germany, France, and Switzerland are making different arguments about the development of movable metal type, there is not an agreed on opinion. There are two clear facts: "The oldest existing book printed by movable metal type was printed in Cheongju, Korea, and the book is housed in the National Library of France;" and "From the cultural historical perspective, Gutenberg's movable metal type significantly impacted European society and contributed to the Reformation and the Industrial Revolution[7]." The development of Gutenberg's movable metal type was from the realization that coin-producing technology and a press machine could be used to make movable type with metal. However, his movable metal type is well

---

7) Kim, Seung-hwan, "Creation of New Jikji Culture," *Printing and Publishing Culture*, Cheongju Early Printing Museum, 2000. p.124.

preserved in Maintz, Germany, and a number of the 42-line Bibles are preserved as well.

Korea—the proud developer of the movable metal type which was used to print *Jikji*, the oldest extant metal print book in the world—needs to respect such objective facts. In particular, it should show its respect for the cultural eye of France as it currently possesses and appreciates *Jikji*. At the same time, it should also acknowledge the value of the movable metal type of Gutenberg from Germany, which was used to print the 42-line Bibles and contributed to the mass production and distribution of information. *Jikji* is not a looted cultural property. It was moved to France and housed in the National Library of France through proper processes and procedures. It is not an appropriate response for Korea to request its repatriation. The value of *Jikji* can be raised in the world's cultural history only when Korea, the nation that printed it, cooperates with France, the nation that possesses it. It is would wise for Korea to respect the historic value of Gutenberg's movable metal type. If his 42-line Bibles are valuable in that they contributed to the mass production of knowledge, Korea's *Jikji* is important in that it contains reverent spiritual value.[8]

---

8) Kim, Seung-hwan, "Creation of New Jikji Culture," *Printing and Publishing Culture*, Cheongju Early Printing Museum, 2000. p.125.

III

Jikji, Registered in the Memory of the World and
Cheongju, the Birthplace of Early Printing

1. The Cultural and Historical Meaning of *Jikji*

In 1911, Henri Vever, a French jeweler, bought *Jikji* for 180 francs at an auction held at Hotel Drouot. He could buy the book at a low price because it was put up for auction and was underestimated because nobody knew what value and meaning that the book had. After he died in 1943, according to the wishes in Henri's will, *Jikji* was donated to the National Library of France. This is how it was ended up being housed in the Oriental Manuscript Room in the National Library of France. Then, why was it moved to France? On June 4, 1886, Korea, or Joseon back then, and France concluded a commercial treaty that touched upon various issues including friendship, trade, commerce, and exchange between the two nations. The original name of the treaty was the Treaty of Friendship, Commerce and Navigation between France and Corea, which is Seoul local tangible cultural asset No.112 and was housed in the National Library of Korea as a diplomatic document from the end of the Joseon dynasty.

Under the treaty, Victor Collin de Plancy (1853-1922) came to Korea from China as the first French Minister to Korea. He was deeply interested in bibliographies and calligraphy and started to collect all kinds of materials in Joseon. Plancy asked his interpreter, Morris Courant, to arrange his collection including *Jikji*, and Courant wrote in his book, "The oldest known Korean book printed with molded movable type, in 1377." In 1893, Plancy returned to France with Lee, Shim, a dancer King Gojong gave to him as a present, but came back to Korea when he was reappointed as the French Minister from 1896 to 1906. On his return to France, he shipped all of his collections from Korea including *Jikji*. *Jikji*, which had been forgotten for a long time, drew attention in 1972, when it appeared at a book exhibition in Paris during the "International Book Year," because it was Korea's oldest extant metal printed book, and it turned out to be the world's oldest. Dr. Park, Byung-sun, who was working as a librarian at the National Library of France, rediscovered the meaning and value of the book.

When she found the book in 1972, she paid attention to the passage at the end of *Jikji*—"*Seongwang chilnyeon jeongsa chilwol il cheongjumok oe heungdeoksa jujainsi* (宣光七年 丁巳七月 日 淸州牧 外 興德寺 鑄字印 施, which said it was printed with metal movable type in July 1377 at Heungdeoksa Temple near Cheongju). In order to prove that the book was printed with movable metal type, she verified that the letters had a unique metal form which were not shown in letters from woodblock printing or manually transcribed. Then, she submitted it to the book fair in 1972 to surprise the world. The exhibited book (the second volume of *Jikji*) was printed on folded white paper (24.6×17.0 cm) with a new yellow cover on which "*Jikji*" was printed. The original title is "*Baegun hwasang chorok buljo jikjisimcheyojeol*" (白雲和尚抄錄佛祖直指心體要節, the second volume of "Anthology of Great Buddhist Priests' Zen Teachings)," and was called "*Buljo jikjisimcheyojeol*" or "*Jikji*" for short. Its original text was a hand-written copy of an abstract by Baegun Hwasang (白雲和尚, 1299-1374), who was the king's teacher at the end of the Goryeo dynasty, in 1372 (the 21st year of King Gongmin). The hand-written manuscript was printed with movable metal type by Seokchan (釋璨) and Daljam (達湛), the disciples of Beakun, with offerings from a female priest, Myodeok (妙德), at Heungdeoksa Temple in Cheongju. The wax casting method was known to be used to cast movable type to print *Jikji*, and due to the characteristics of Chinese characters as an isolated language, the characters themselves were cast instead of casting and typesetting vowels and consonants like alphabets.

In 1985, the site of Heungdeoksa Temple, in which *Jikji* was printed, was excavated and later designated as a Memory of the World by UNESCO on September 4, 2001. *Jikji* is a kind of textbook, which contains selected sermons of Mahayana Buddhist sages and Seon (禪,

Zen) masters. The most important content would be "*Jikji insim gyungseong seongbul*" (直指人心見性成佛, directly pointing to the heart and seeing into self-nature to attain the Buddhahood or become a Buddha), which means that "if you find the good-natured essence of your mind to see the truth, you can become a Buddha." This is a teaching of Musimseon (無心禪, Mushin Zen) through emptied mind and Ganhwaseon (看話禪, Kanhwa Zen) through topics of Zen Buddhism, a mixture of Indian Mahayana Buddhism and Taoism. *Jikji* is very important in the religious as well as cultural senses. This is because it is the world's oldest extant book printed with movable metal type. The importance of movable metal type was proven by *Life* magazine when it put "Gutenberg's Bible printing" in first place for the most important 100 events and 100 persons for the past millennium (1001-2000), which meant that Gutenberg's "42-line Bibles" had an profound impact on human history. Metal movable-type printing, which was spread by many people including Gutenberg, disseminated knowledge throughout Europe, including Switzerland, France, Germany, Italy, and UK. The movable type changed the printing technique from transcription on parchment to the revolutionary printing by press after typesetting movable metal type pieces with matrices for mass duplication.

This brought about many changes in science and technology, law, education, art, and transportation. Authority was taken away from the ruling class, who monopolized religion and knowledge, and the newly emerged citizen class (bourgeois) came to take the lead in history. As a result, metal movable type printing became a turning point in human history because it had great influence on the Reformation (1517) led by Martin Luther and the Industrial Revolution that took place across Europe. At the same time, it gave rise to the Renaissance, spread human-centered humanism, and contributed to the development of capitalism. Movable metal type is important because of the significant meaning it had and it is meaningful that Korea was the nation that developed and used movable metal type for the first time in the world. Nonetheless, the movable metal type of Korea and that of Gutenberg have different historical contexts in that it is not Korea's technology but Gutenberg's that directly impacted human history. *Jikji*, which was printed by Korean metal movable type, is important because it proves the development of the world's oldest movable metal type, and Korea's invention is meaningful for the spiritual values that printing in small quantity has. This leads to the question: What is *Jikji's* spiritual meaning?

2. The Spiritual Meaning of *Jikji*

Jikji was not a product for mass production. It was printed in small quantities to elevate the spiritual values. The first purpose of the publication of *Jikji* was to move toward an enlightened world through the cultivation of the spirit, and the second was to publish textbooks for education and learning. For these two purposes, Myodeok, the sponsor, and Seokchan and Daljam, the publishers, made sacred efforts, and many others sincerely participated in the publication of *Jikji*. Since casting movable metal type and printing on paper were very difficult techniques, it would have been difficult to publish *Jikji*, if it had not been for the spirit of experimentation. If Gutenberg's Bible symbolizes the Christianity culture, *Jikji* symbolizes the Buddhism culture. It was possible to print *Jikji* because many people endeavored to do it with the dedication of their body and mind for Buddha with sincerity. Then, what does the word "*jikji*" in the title mean?

Jikji's headword, *Jikji insim gyeongseong seongbul* ("*jikji*": directly pointing, "insim": human mind, "*gyeonseong*": seeing into self-nature, *seongbul*: attaining the Buddhahood or becoming a Buddha) means "to see the heart straight to find the true nature of Buddha and become a being like Buddha." Then, what is the true nature of Buddha? Both *Bul* (佛) and *Bulta* (浮陀) refers to Buddha. They are transliteration of Buddha meaning "sentient beings" or "sentience" in Sanskrit. Since *Bul* in *Seongbul* is already in the mind, it requires cultivation to directly see the heart. *Seon* (禪, Zen) is most important among many cultivation methods. There are two kinds of Seon: 1) *Mukjoseon* (黙照禪) to reach a freedom in the state of a peaceful mind and at the stage of no-mind and no-thought, mindfulness and non-perception; and 2) *Ganhwaseon* (看話禪) to reach the final state by thoroughly and deeply studying the given word for contemplation. *Jikji insim gyungseong seongbul* is a concept that implies achieving *seongbul through jikji,* a way of *Seon.* In particular, *jikji* is a method of Seon emphasized by *Musimseon* among *Mukjoseon* methods.

Then, what enlightenment can be obtained from *jikji insim* (pointing directly to the mind or enlightenment without recourse to conceptual thought or letters) and *gyeongseong seongbul*? The essence to be learned by directly pointing the mind is *Seongbul*, but what is important is the process and content of *Gyeonseong*. One of the expressions that represents the process and contents of *Gyeongseong* is "Form is nothing other than emptiness; emptiness is nothing other than form." A plain interpretation might be "something that exists is something that does not exist, and something that does not exist is something that exists," and it also means something bright and dark, something alive and dead, and something neither clean nor dirty. This double-sided phenomenon is emptiness and emptiness is also fullness. It is a contradiction in formal logic, but it is really not, according to Madhyamaka of Nagarjuna, an Indian Buddhist scholar. In the universe, a myriad of particulars, forms, or things relate to each other in a relative way, "Something can exist without existing, and something does not exist while existing" is possible. However, the truth is in the mind. Then, what can be obtained by enlightening "something that can exist without existing, and something does not exist while existing" in the mind?

What is earned from enlightenment is the truth that a myriad of particulars, forms, or things in the universe including oneself are all temporary phenomenon. All the agonies and delusions are coming from the mind, and the mind should be well subdued to remove discrimination in mind and to reach the original state of a calm mind. In particular, it should be realized that the temporary oneself and the essence of the universe is one. This means "the oneself exists without existing" and at the same time, the essence and the oneself is one being. In other words, the "absence of oneself" means that the oneself is "absent" from an infinite space-time perspective, but it "exists" in reality. When "myself," the being that exists in the present, understands that "Form is nothing other than emptiness; emptiness is nothing other than form," the oneself disappears and is integrated into the universal essence. This is the continuance of the tradition of "oneness or unity of atman (oneself) and brahman (universal principle). This is "the mind itself is the Buddha," expressed in a special transmission outside scriptures and non-dependence on words and letters. Then, what is the method for *jikjiinsim gyeonseongseongbul*?

Gyojong (the doctrinal school in contrast to Seon or Zen Buddhism) is centered on gradual cultivation, which means to study scriptures and learn theories to reach enlightenment. *Seonjong* (the Dhyana School or Seon Buddhism) is focused on sudden enlightenment through deep contemplation and medication to see the essence of the mind. *Jikji*, the primary point of Seon, means to see directly into the mind with introspective insight. The key of Seon is *Jikjiinsim gyeonseongseongbul*. The phrase, "See straight into one's own mind and become a Buddha based on the essence of the inner self" is the cultivation method still upheld by modern-day Buddhist ascetics. As discussed above, *Jikji* is a treasure for humankind that contains spiritual value for education, experiment, and piety.

3. Cheongju, the Birthplace of *Jikji*

Jikji is one of the things that symbolizes Cheongju, but what expresses the city best is the "song of Cheongju Citizens," composed by Younghi Pagh-Paan, a world-class composer currently working in Germany, and to which Cheongju citizens wrote the lyrics for together. She recalled that she decided to become a composer after she listened to *Korea Fantasy* by Ahn, Eak-tai when she was a third grader at a middle school in Cheongju.

The composer has won numerous awards including the 1st Prize at the Rostrum of Composers (UNESCO) in Paris, France, and became a member of the Akademie der Künste, Berlin. Although she worked in Germany, she always missed and loved her hometown of Cheongju, and Korea, her mother country, and it would be her love for her homeland that inspired her to compose the song. The song is simple, but it captures well the history of Cheongju and the sentiment of Cheongju citizens as it describes the beautiful natural environment of the city.

Sangdang, the destination of gentle breezes, the home of wide fields and straight roads, splendid culture flourished, the light of history will be lit up for the bright future of this place, ah, Cheongju, the land of happiness, you will be loved forever.

The fertile Mihocehon plain, noble-mindedness like the clear blue sky, the birthplace of Jikji, the cultural heritage of people across the world who will realize their hopes and dreams. ah, Cheongju, the land of happiness, you will be loved forever.

This song emphasizes "*Jikji*, the cultural heritage of people across the world," which reveals the pride that Cheongju has for being the place where *Jikji* was printed. The song starts with the word, "Sangdang." What is Sangdang? When Cheongju which was *Mahan* (馬韓, a loose confederacy of statelets that existed from around the 1st century BC to the 5th century AD) in ancient times and a territory of Baekje (a kingdom that existed from 18 BCE–660 CE), it was called "*Sangdanghyeon*" (上堂縣) or "*Nangbiseong*". In 685, after Silla united the three kingdom, Cheongju was called "*Seowonsogyeong*"

142

(西原小京) meaning the "capital in the west" of Unified Silla. At that time, Cheongju was in the central part of what is currently Chungcheongnamdo and the southwestern part of Chungcheongbukdo. The name was changed to Cheongju in 940, when the name first appeared in history, and became Cheongjumok in 983. The area was first named Chungcheongdo in 1106, and Cheongju, together with Chungju, were important places in the area.

After Joseon was founded, its territory was divided into eight provinces (道 do) in 1413, and Gongjumok, Cheongjumok, Chungjumok, and Hongjumok (currently Hongseonggun) were established in Chungcheongdo. The concept of locality around Chungju and Cheongju was established when thirteen provinces were established in 1896, when Chungcheongdo was divided into Chungcheongnamdo and Chungcheongbukdo, and the provincial office was established in Chungju. In 1908, the provincial office was moved to Cheongju, and on October 1,1910, under the Japanese rule, the provincial government was moved to Cheongju, which made it the center of Chungcheongbukdo. Therefore, the historical meaning of Cheongju may be found in its relationship with Chungju. In 1946, Cheongjubu and Cheongwongun were separated, and Cheongju became Cheongju city in 1949, and once again on July 1, 2014, Cheongju city and Cheongwongun were merged into the current Cheongju city. Cheongju is the capital of Chungcheongbukdo and located at the center of the Chungcheong area. It shares its boundaries with Sejong city, Daejeon city, as well as Boeun, Jincheon, Jeungpyeong, and Okcheon in Chungcheongbukdo. Geographically, Miho Stream, a tributary of the Geum River, flows through the city, east of the city is mountainous, and its west boasts plain with small hills. It is well expressed in the Chungcheongbukdo Culture Charter.

Clear winds blow along the Baekdudaegan mountain range. When the sun sets in the west, the bright moon rises in the east. Here, where culture was cultivated with a fresh breeze and a bright moon and art was enriched with merriment and mirth, is the center of Korea, Chungcheongbukdo. People of Chungbuk, with their mild and integral dispositions, especially loved the culture and arts that brilliantly flourished in the culture of the State's central area[9].

The Governor of Chungcheongbukdo and the minister of Culture, Sports and Tourism declared the Chungcheongbukdo Culture Charter at a ceremony to celebrate the 2008 Korean Culture Day held in Cheongju. Since Cheongju is the provincial capital of Chungcheongbukdo,

---

9) Chungcheongbukdo Culture Charter, 2008.
   Clear winds blow along the Baekdudaegan mountain range. When the sun sets in the west, the bright moon rises in the east. Here, where culture was cultivated with a fresh breeze and a bright moon and art was enriched with merriment and mirth, is the center of Korea, Chungcheongbukdo. People of Chungbuk, with their mild and integral dispositions, especially loved the culture and arts that brilliantly flourished in the culture of the State's central area.

the cultural characteristics of Chungcheongbukdo are those of Cheongju. The charter stressed that Cheongju has the symbolic status of cheongpungmyeongwol (清風明月, a fresh breeze and a bright moon) and has loved and cultivated culture and arts. Of course, the charter set the creativity and the spirit of experiment of *Jikji* as important values.

This historical background has formed the identity of Cheongju. Cheongju has the characteristics that match its name, clean village. Due to this proximity to Gaeseong—the capital of Goryeo, and Hanseong—the capital of Joseon, it has several other characteristics of being a center of a nation. When "Mangseonnu Pavilion," which holds the historical tradition of Cheongju, was moved, the characteristics of the city were set as loyalty, fidelity, gentleness, and modesty. The "Written Prayer for the Roof Raising Ritual for Relocated and Restored Mangseonnu Pavilion" describes Cheongju as "the place called by different names including Sangdang, Nangseong, and Seowon, where the Baekdudaegan mountain area, which has the spirit of the Korean people, is located to the east, and the Geum River flows in the west with the west wind blowing along the river with auspicious energy all around it." It shows that the "Cheonjuity," the identity of Cheongju, is its orientation toward a sense of stability, the characteristics of an inland area, resistance, adaptation to the natural law, normality, moderation, and a sense of balance.

Historically, Cheongju represents the spirit and the characteristics of Chungcheongdo. A safe description of Chungcheongdo would be: "The mountains and rivers are smooth and beautiful and it has become a place where the gentry lives due to its proximity to Gyeongseong. Since most noble families in Gyeongseong owned land and property here and its customs are not different from that of Gyeongseong, it is the most appropriate place to live" is actually a description of Cheongju. The identity of Cheongju, revealed through its symbolic images, is a city of culture and art that meets the demands of its people in an era of globalization, because it is the birthplace of global printing culture where *Jikji* was printed with the metal movable type. The Cheongju Citizen Charter explains that "Cheongju has maintained its leadership role in ideology and academic pursuits as a historic cultural city[10]." Cheongju's symbols are the "*Jikji*," Sangdang Sanseong Fortress, Cheongju Platanus Road, Cheongju Early Printing Museum, Uamsan Mountain, Yongdusaji Archeological Site, Seongan-gil, Yukgeori Traditional Market, Central Park, and Cheongju International Craft Biennale. The images associated with Cheongju are a city of education, Cheongju Platanus Road, *Jikji*, clean, Musim stream, Sangdang Sanseong Fortress, a city of culture (art), a city of history (tradition), a city of transportation, and a city of the gentry class.

---

10) The Cheongju Citizen Charter, Sangdang park

IV

The UNESCO Memory Program

The UNESCO Memory of the World is a cultural memory program. Although memories are different from records, documentary heritages and memory heritages can be understood similarly in that things are remembered through records. "The effect of inscription on the Memory of the World Register is as follows: it is possible to prepare for the development into a legal entity that can be protected internationally, receive UNESCO technical support for preservation, and use the emblem of the Memory of the World and continuously promote it via UNESCO's website[11]." However, the subject of memory, set by UNESCO, is not a single people or citizens of a nation, but global citizens. It is important that global citizens remember *Jikji* and share its meaning and value. What is the exact concept of memory? What is the meaning of cultural memory that *Jikji* has? Why is the collective memory of global citizens important?

---

11) Early Printing Museum, Cheongju, Chungbuk, Korea
http://jikjiworld.cheongju.go.kr/jikjiworld/contents.do?key=17513

1. Memory

Remembering is a mental action that allows individuals and groups to preserve and recall something that happened in the past inside and outside consciousness. Memory is important in many ways and without memory, learning would be impossible. In short, memory is created in a process of input, storage, output, and recognition. Input means that information is put in the brain; storage means memories are being stored in the brain; output means what is stored comes across one's mind; and recognition means confirming the memory again. However, memory works mostly through the activities of neurons and functions of brain cells. Synapses of sensory neurons recognize external information and deliver it to the brain through central nerves. In this process, working memory encrypts memories and sorts them into explicit and implicit memories. The brain analyzes the information and re-sorts by area. The hippocampus of the human brain stores spatial and explicit memories, while the amygdala stores emotions and implicit memories.

How memories are stored and recalled depends on the type of memory. Memory can be divided into three types by time: ultra-short-term sensory memories related to visual, auditory and olfactory senses; short-term memories to be retained for a relatively short time; and long-term memories to be remembered for a long time.

John Robert Anderson (1947-), a psychologist, classified long-term memories into two types by pattern: declarative and procedural memories. The former is also divided into two types: semantic memories and episodic memories[12]. Semantic memories are related to value and meaning, for example, "Rome was the capital of the Roman Empire, and a city on the lower Tevere River, in the mid-part of Italy." Episodic memories remember emotions and an episode, such as "The coin that I threw into Trevi Fountain will still be there."

Second, non-declarative or implicit memories are memories that are automatically recalled, such as the ability to ride a bicycle or swim. If things are not remembered, the same mistakes would be repeated over and over again. However, what is important is not what was first remembered but what remained as a memory because memory controls consciousness, and builds relationships through common memories. That is why we sometimes struggle for a memory and forget what took place surrounding a memory. In fact, forgetting is also as important as remembering. According to a psychological study of memory retention curves, the memory loss rate after 24 hours was estimated at around 33%. The forgetting curve plummeted in a day or two, the rest was slowly forgotten, and only those stored as long-term memories survived to the last. In particular, memories

---

12) John Robert Anderson, *Language, Memory, and Thought*, (Hillsdale, New Jersey: Lawrence Erlbaum Associates, 1976).

related to emotions and sentiments are highly likely to be long-term memories. This means that emotions and sentiments are stored for a long time as memory traces or engrams.

Remembering is mostly recalling the past, but sometimes it predicts the future, like remembering a promise. However, ultra-short-term, short-term, and long-term memories, in many cases, are influenced by temporal and spatial conditions, physiological and physiological differences, and social circumstances, and are especially dependent on the existence of emotion. This means that memories, in fact, are not maintained as is, but processed as needed. That is why Freud said that for negative memories, defense mechanisms work or intentional regression happens. It is a self-centered response that creates autobiographical memories by distorting and reinforcing the memory. For example, people sorting out memories for what to remember and what not to reinforces the justification for things to remember, and forms a collective consciousness, a memory community, through collective memories. Then, what does a group remember?

2. Collective Memory

Jikji is the world's oldest extant metal movable type print book, which led to both Korea and UNESCO undertaking various projects to remember and commemorate it together with people around the world. UNESCO inscribed *Jikji* on the Memory of the World Register, a list of things worth remembering and commemorating with people around the world. However, the designation and commemoration of a cultural heritage item should be done as part of a certain social framework. Then, what are social frameworks of memory, and what do individuals and groups remember? Remembering is a mental action which allows individuals and groups to preserve and recall something that happened in the past. Yet, the memory of an individual and that of a group can be different since the former is an action of the nervous system and the brain while the latter is an action of will and awareness. Neither individuals nor groups can remember everything nor do they try to do so. In particular, a group sorts out memories and remembers what should be remembered. In this process, social frameworks, i.e. values and standards, come into play.

According to Maurice Halbwachs (1877-1945), a French sociologist, in a society, there are frames of its way of thinking, perspectives, positions, customs, and value orientation, and memory is decided in such a framework. If an individual remembers things outside the range of social memory, the individual is separated and ostracized from the society. Therefore, memory is the basis of group identity beyond a social phenomenon. This is why he asked, "What binds the group and the society?" and answered, "It is memory." According to him, memory controls consciousness and binds a group and a society. At the same time, memory is reorganized and combined by social frameworks, but it also constitutes social frameworks. Memory and social frameworks interact with each other to integrate a society's values, ideology, objectives, and emotions, which makes a society a community of memory. This community of memory has something in common with the imagined community that Benedict Anderson mentioned.

Unlike the imagined community being a community based on imagination, a community of memory is different in than it is a community that is based on memory created by reorganizing and combining facts. Because of this, the same event can be remembered differently based on the way of remembering. Therefore, individuals who have the same way of remembering and the same meaning of a memory form a group and share a consciousness. By definition, a group is a community set by certain criteria and pursues a common interest. A group sharing the same memories has its own way of communicating. The memory of an individual is recollected and recognized through the memory of the group that is then shared with the other individuals[13]. This is why Halbwachs understood a group and a society from the perspective of relationships, and

13) Maurice Halbwachs, *The collective memory*, (New York: Harper & Row Colophon Books, 1980), p.31.

emphasized communication. Members, who are in the relationship of communication, share communicative memories centered on places and incidents. This means that "for communicative memory, the way of remembering and the content of the memory is the same." From this perspective, a group or a society, such as families, neighbors, towns, and peoples, are communicative communities.

A group is an organization formed through engaging in communication and building relationships. Each group has memories that its members share. Halbwachs named it collective memory. It is memories of experiences in the past, knowledge, and information shared by the group. His collective memory concept evolved from the collective consciousness concept of his teacher, Emile Durkheim. A set is a collection of elements with the same properties under certain conditions. The active collective consciousness that belongs to the same set forms a sense of solidarity. Durkheim explained that collective effervescence amplifies common emotions and experiences, and has a powerful force. Halbwachs believed that Durkheim's collective consciousness and collective effervescence make up the consciousness of the group, and collective memory works during the process of forming collective consciousness. Hence, a group completes, shares, combines, and distributes memories in order to have social relationships. In this sense, collective memory is an active will and a social practice.

Collective memory implies "Remember!" an instruction of struggle for memory. The command, "remember" also contains another command, "Forget other things!" This explains how selected and reconstructed facts are remembered instead of the facts as they were. Therefore, how and what to be remembered is more important than the actual fact. This is how subjective and personal experiences are integrated with objective and collective experiences. Even what is not experienced can be remembered by social consensus. For example, throughout the 21st century Koreans do not have direct experiences with wartime sex slavery (known as "comfort women"), but it is remembered as an important memory because of Korean social frameworks, "Remember comfort women!" Incidents and emotions recognized by a group become long-term memories that have authority. However, collective memory continuously changes depending on the time and circumstances. In this regard, a memory can be more vivid and dynamic than history.

3. Cultural Memory

Memory is what an individual and a group preserve and recollect about something that happened in the past inside and outside consciousness. Memory is a mental function that living things have and is both a process and a method. Human beings learned how to survive and build a civilized society through memory and learning.

Jan Assmann, who stressed the social meaning of memory, emphasized cultural memory among all the types of memories. He classified memory into individual memory, communicative memory, and cultural memory. Individual memory is subjective memory that works in the neural network of an individual, and communicative memory is a memory of daily communication that works in social frameworks, while cultural memory is memory that works in a historic and mythic frames of time and is the basis for cultural identity[14]. Cultural memory is formed in over a long time of history, and functions as canon because it is not only socially agreed upon but also endlessly reproduced and passed down after obtaining cultural meaning.

The core of cultural memory is that memories are culturally reconstructed, function as cultural symbols, and cultural practices are carried out based on it. Jan Assmann's cultural memory emphasizes collective memory of culture, among his teacher, Halbwachs' collective memories. Halbwachs created the concept of collective consciousness by furthering Durkheim's collective consciousness. Based on the fact that there are distortions and flaws in human memories, he inquired on "what and how a group remembers". He thought that the memories

---

14) Jan Assmann, "Communicative and Cultural Memory", *Cultural Memory Studies. An International and interdisciplinary Handbook*, (Berlin and New York, 2008), p.109.

of a group were reconstructed by social frameworks and from the perspective of the present. Such memory theories of Durkheim and Halbwachs greatly influenced Assmann. He studied the patterns of cultural memories, thinking collective memories acquire meaning and values through cultural practice. According to him, festivals, rituals, narratives, poems, images and other cultural elements form the islands of time. The islands of time are imprinted as memories through retrospective contemplativeness. Objectification takes place at the same time.

Assmann's concept of cultural memory reinforces a group identity, reconstitutes recognition, is objectified and forms transparent communication, systematizes a system and an institution, suggests norms through differences and values, and introspects self-images and cultural memories[15]. Through all of them, they enhance the cultural memories of a group and establish valuable memories. Cultural memory has the character of canon because it rules the consciousness of a group over a long period of time. It is passed down through a variety of cultural media and symbols—for example, awards, memorial halls, symbolic sculptures, records, literary texts, museums, tour souvenirs, photos, gifts, reproductions of famous

---

15) Jan Assmann, "Collective memory and Cultural Identity", *New German Critique*, no 65, Cultural History/Cultural Studies, (Spring-Summer, 1995). pp.130-131.

paintings are the media of cultural memories. In this process, the knowledge and experiences of a group are culturally reinterpreted and culturally shared to be imprinted as collective memory and the collective consciousness that Halbwachs proposed, or evolve into the collective unconscious of Carl Gustav Jung.

Aleida Assmann, the wife and colleague of Jan Assmann, created a concept of cultural memories focused on space and place. According to her, art and technology are something to be remembered and long-term memories are to be remembered for a long time. Certain places generate a meaning of space for memory. The Assmanns said that cultural memories themselves were cultural practices. The key point of the Assmanns' and many scholars' discussions on collective memory and cultural memory is that "the present culturally reconstructs the past, and the reconstructed cultural memories again form the present." While history pursues the overall and objective description, memories have vitality and dynamic forces, even though they are fragmentary and subjective. Of course, history is a form of memory and history itself is reconstructed by the spirit of the time and the view of history. However, memories are different from history in that they are newly constructed and gain diverse meanings through social practices.

V

The Patterns of Jikji's Cultural Memory

1. Cultural Memory 1—The Campaign to Bring Jikji Back and the Cheongju Early Printing Museum

Cheongju citizens expected that *Jikji*, housed in France, would have been preserved in Korea as well because they believed the precious metal movable type print would have been left in temples or book repositories. With this expectation in mind, they ceaselessly carried out *Jikji*-related projects including the establishment of the Cheongju Early Printing Museum in March 1992 as well as the restoration of Heungdeoksa Temple. In particular, the Citizens of Cheongju decided to form a "Headquarters to Bring *Jikji* Back to Korea" at the 14th Plenary Session of the Executive Committee on November 8, 1996. A signboard hanging ceremony was held on January 15, 1997, and the headquarters started its operation in earnest after the opening ceremony on March 25. The headquarters requested cooperation from the Cultural Heritage Administration and the Buddhist community, including the Jogye Order of Korean Buddhism and the Korean Buddhist Taego Order, and it also requested to the Ministry of Education that *Jikji*-related subjects be put in textbooks, while asking for support and cooperation from the Korean Publishers Association and the Korean Printers Association. Although the name was changed from the Citizens of Cheongju to Citizens' Solidarity for Participation & Autonomy of Chungbuk on January 8, 2001 at the 13th General Conference of the Citizens of Cheongju, it has continued its campaign to bring *Jikji* back.

In 1985, the site of Heungdeoksa Temple was excavated, and after it was designated as one of the important historical sites in Korea in 1986, Cheongju city and its citizens passionately started their efforts to bring *Jikji* back. The Cheongju Early Printing Museum, established on March 17, 1992, held many domestic and international symposiums and *Jikji*-related events and conducted the campaign to bring *Jikji* back to Korea. Previous Cheongju mayors, including Na, Gi-jeong, Kim, Hyeon-soo, Han, Dae-soo, Nam, Sang-woo, Han, Beom-deok, and Lee, Seoung-soon made efforts for construction of facilities and the globalization of *Jikji*. For their part, previous governors of Chungcheongbukdo such as Lee, Won-jong, Jeong, Woo-taek, and Lee, Si-gong, worked hard to the raise its value. Cheongju city set up an ordinance for the operation of projects to support the campaign to bring *Jikji* back to Korea in January 2006 to provide institutional support for its safe return in a timely manner. As a result of such efforts, *Jikji* and the Cheongju Early Printing Museum were included in the Korean reading textbook for fifth graders of elementary school in 2012. In the following year, the Cheongju Metal Type Casting Succession Hall, established in 2013, has been fulfilling its function as an agency specialized in casting and demonstrating movable metal type. It is the Cheongju Early Printing Museum that institutionalizes such memories. The museum is involved in many programs as Korea's most important museum specializing in early printing and it is also a think tank.

People of Cheongju and Chungcheongbukdo endowed *Jikji* with special meaning and undertook many projects to remember it. Cheongju citizens held numerous art events in dance, music, the theater, literature, and calligraphy including *the Opera Jikji*, which premiered in the Sejong Center for the Performing Arts in Seoul on September 22, 2000. They also held speeches, debates, and essay contests on *Jikji*, international Jikji cycle competitions, Jikji marathons, Jikji international dance sports competitions, Jikji Cup handball tournaments, Jikji basketball tournaments, Jikji soccer tournaments, Jikji billiards competitions, Jikji foot volleyball competitions, and other Jikji-related sporting events to promote Jikji. In particular, the headquarters toured Buddhist temples across Korea and went to China, following traces of Baekun hwasang who compiled the contents of *Jikji*, to find more copies of *Jikji*. All of these efforts were to recreate *Jikji* and give it even more meaning. Although they could not find it, Cheongju citizens came to love it and recognize it as "a proud asset of the Korean people" through such activities. Korean people also came to know more about its value and meaning. The efforts and desire of Cheongju citizens to find and remember *Jikji* were themselves an important cultural citizen movement that should be remembered.

2. Cultural Memory 2—The Jikji Globalization Declaration

Cheongju has made efforts in many ways to remember and preserve *Jikji* and to raise an awareness of its world cultural heritage not only among Cheongju citizens but also among people across the globe. In particular, the city held an international printing and publishing fair in 2000. In order to give this international meaning, the World Jikji Cultural Association was established in 2005, as part of an effort to let Koreans and people across the globe remember *Jikji*. The subjects of this collective memory are not only Koreans but people across the globe, so Cheongju has been putting in great effort to make *Jikji* known by people across the globe. One of the examples that demonstrates such effort is the Jikji Globalization Declaration on June 15, 2004. The following is the declaration.

Jikji, the oldest existing metal printing type in the world, was published in 1377 in Cheongju and is kept as a unique book in the Manuscript Orianteaux of France National Library. It was rediscovered in 1972 in

France. The Buddhist temple, which was the birth place of Jikji, was excavated in 1984. From that time, the citizens of Cheongju have made every effort and have made lots of progress. As a result of these endeavors, Jikji was registered as a Memory of the World and it was decided to confer the Jikji Prize under the authority of UNESCO. Now, it is time to make known to all the value and spirit of Jikji. The universalization of Jikji will be launched with a cultural strategy, informational strategy, and industrial strategy. Let's open the spiritual mind, and create a new paradigm for education with Jikji. Let's make a new scientific and cultural phase with Jikji. Let's sincerely spread the light to make Cheongju into a base for a new civilization.

The metal printing type of Jikji, which was invented by the Korean people's devotion, is the most important expression of this precious cultural capital. This priceless object has the value of creation, the value of education, the value of history, the value of knowledge, and the value of art and culture. Also, Jikji carries the meaning of equality, sincerity, the sharing of knowledge, modesty, benevolence, peace, sacrifice, piety, petition, and emancipation. However, we should realize that Koreans cannot develop the original value and its meaning successfully on their own. Jikji has not yet contributed enough to civilization and to world history. With such regret and reflection in mind, we will be launching a new idea of civilization towards every corner of the world.

We must bear in mind that shallow globalization is a trap for humankind. For that reason, we reject globalization as a centralization of power and monopoly over all the things. On the contrary, we will orient towards cultural diversity and multiculturalism. Through such a humanistic retrospection and an ecological viewpoint, we can promote the thought of Jikji in this global village. In this context, Jikji would be a symbol of coexistence and harmony. Deconstructing the contradictions of the age, we are going to reconstruct a new civilization. Humankind can become sustainable and promote development and cultural diversity through these efforts. Above all, we will respect the meaningful Gutenberg printing culture and will give thanks to the cultural earnestness of the French. As a matter of course, we love all other countries' cultures, including those of China, Japan, Russia, Spain, etc. With the hope of mutual cooperation, we suggest opening a new age of civilization. This small step will lead to a big process in the near future. The conciliation of all regional cultures, ethnic cultures, and geo-culture is the real intention of Jikji. Herein, as one unified planet of homo-sapiens, we deliver this declaration toward the past and the future. We carry the hope for harmony with every single world citizen in the world system[16].

---

16) Declaration of Jikji Globalization, Jun, 15, 2004.
   The Jikji, the oldest existing metal printing type in the world, was published in 1377 in Choengju and is kept as a unique book in the Manuscrit Orianteaux of France National Library. It was rediscovered in 1972 in France. The Buddhist temple, which was the birth place of Jikji, was excavated in 1984. From that time, the citizens of Cheongju

The values of *Jikji* emphasized in the declaration are the values of creation, education, the dissemination of knowledge, civilization, culture, information sharing and dissemination, and art. The

have made every effort and have made lots of progress. As a result of these endeavors, the Jikji was registered as a Memory of the World and it was decided to confer on the Jikji Prize under the authority of UNESCO. Now, it is time to make known to all the value and spirit of the Jikji. The universalization of the Jikji will be launched with a cultural strategy, informational strategy, and industrial strategy. Let's open the spiritual mind, and create a new paradigm for education with the Jikji. Let's make a new scientific and cultural phase with the Jikji. Let's sincerely spread the light to make Cheongju into a base for a new civilization. The metal printing type of the Jikji, which was invented by the Korean's devotion, is the most important expression of this precious cultural capital. This priceless object has the value of creation, the value of education, the value of history, the value of knowledge, and the value of art and culture. Also, the Jikji carries the meaning of equality, sincerity, the sharing of knowledge, modesty, benevolence, peace, sacrifice, piety, petition, and emancipation. However, we should realize that Koreans cannot develop the original value and its meaning successfully on their own. The Jikji has not yet contributed enough to civilization and to world history. With such a regret and reflection in mind, we will be launching a new idea of civilization towards every corner of the world. We must bear in mind that shallow globalization is a trap for humankind. For that reason, we reject globalization as centralization of power and monopoly over all the things. On the contrary, we will orient towards cultural diversity and multi-culturalism. Through such a humanistic retrospection and an ecological viewpoint, we can promote the thought of the Jikji in this global village. In this context, the Jikji would be a symbol of coexistence and harmony. Deconstructing the contradictions of the age, we are going to reconstruct a new civilization. Humankind can become sustainable and promote development and cultural diversity through these efforts. Above all, we will respect the meaningful Gutenberg printing culture and will give thanks to the cultural earnestness of the French. As a matter of course, we love all other countries' cultures, including those of China, Japan, Russia, Spain, etc. With the hope of mutual cooperation, we suggest opening a new age of civilization. This small step will lead to a big process in the near future. The conciliation of all regional cultures, ethnic cultures and geoculture is the real intention of the Jikji. Herein, as one unified planet of homo-sapiens, we deliver the declaration toward the past and the future. We carry the hope for harmony of every single world-citizen in the world system.

declaration especially stressed that even though *Jikji* was printed in Korea, it was not solely a cultural heritage for Korea but for the entire world. It expressed gratitude to France for its cultural spirit and highly evaluated the meaning and value of Gutenberg's movable metal type. While emphasizing culture and dialogue with culture, it also expressed that it should contribute to the development of cultural history from the past toward the future. It was written based on the universal value of culture and civilization and specified Korea's unique cultural properties. Together with this, the UNESCO/Jikji Memory of the World Prize was created.

3. Cultural Memory 3—The Jikji Prize

Humanity created human civilization through memories, which meant that to remember, learn, and save is the most important human action and responsibility. There are many ways of remembering. Among them, a prize is a valuable object, money, and/or a certificate to compliment an outstanding achievement or very good deed. The prize is awarded to an individual or an organization for commemoration, after screening and deliberation. UNESCO created the Jikji Prize in 2004. The Korean government suggested the prize to UNESCO to commemorate the inscription of *Jikji* on the Memory of the World Register and promote its value in cultural history as well as the purpose of UNESCO's program. UNESCO accepted the proposal and, since then, has presented the prize after it screens and deliberate all the candidates including organizations and institutions that have contributed to the preservation of and access to documentary heritages. The Korean government gives USD 30,000 as an additional prize. From 2005, the prize has been presented to the following awardees every two years.

2005: The National Library of the Czech Republic
2007: The Austrian Audiovisual Research Archive
2009: The National Archives of Malaysia
2011: The National Archives of Australia
2013: ADABI of Mexico
2016: Iberarchivos – ADAI Programme
2018: The National Archives of SAVAMA-DCI in Mali

Most awardees are libraries and archives, which means the methods and processes of preservation are more important than the contents of the records. In other words, "How the document was created and how it has been preserved" is important. As elaborated above, the purpose of the Memory of the World Programme is to increase the accessibility and usability of documentary heritages based on storage and preservation. The Jikji Prize is also intended to better preserve documentary records and their usability by people across the world.

4. Cultural Memory 4—Jikji Festival, Jikji Day, Jikji Intellectual Property Day, and Jikji Korea International festival

Jikji Korea International Festival was started to raise awareness of *Jikji* and let many people from Korea and nations across the world know about Cheongju by participating in the festival. The festival and the Jikji award ceremony have been held in Cheongju, Korea every year from 2004. During the festival, various events from seminars to competitions, exhibitions, and demonstrations of casting movable metal type took place. The Korean government designated

2013 Jikji Award Ceremony

September 4 as "Korean Intellectual Property Day" in December 2017. It is very special to designate a Jikji-related day at the national level. It was an elevation of Jikji Day, which was designated by Cheongju, the birthplace of *Jikji,* to the national level in 2003. The designation was in accordance with Article 29 (1) and (2) of the Framework Act on Intellectual Property, "September fourth shall be designated as Intellectual Property Day to improve citizens' understanding of and interest in the creation, protection, and utilization of intellectual property. The Government will hold a celebration satisfying the purpose of Intellectual Property Day."

The Jikji Korea Festival and the Jikji Award Ceremony was merged into the Jikji Korea International Festival in 2018. This year's slogan was "A global cultural festival which conveys to the world the spirit and the wisdom of *Jikji* and to share them with people across the world."

During the 2018 festival, the International Association of Printing Museums (IAPM) was officially launched. The IAPM is an association of experts who wish to expand the historical and cultural value of printing technology, which has driven the advancement of human civilization, to the future and exchange printing-related information and knowledge. The "Jikji Prize 2.0 Roundtable" was also held to expand the award's meaning and value, and it has been recognized as an excellent award program since its creation in 2001. The roundtable is a venue for documentary culture experts who have received the Jikji Prize gather together to share their expertise and experience while reconfirming the importance of preservation, access, and the utilization of knowledge and promoting international cooperation.

The 2016 Jikji Korea International Festival in 2016 (Streets of Goryeo in 1377)

VI

Conclusion

Humanity achieved civilization through memories. Without memory and learning, mankind would not be living the civilized life it does today. According to Maurice Halbwachs, memory controls consciousness and binds a group and a society. The social frameworks consist of memories, but memories also form the social framework. Memories and the social framework interact with each other to integrate a society's values, ideologies, objectives, and emotions, which means that a society is a community of memories. UNESCO is working hard to create a human community through memories while making efforts for cultural diversity. In the hope that individual people and nations both could work to preserve a variety of cultures, it designates cultural heritages that could be remembered by the entire human race. That is the Memory of the World Programme.

In 2001, UNESCO inscribed the second volume of *Jikji*, printed in 1377, on the Memory of the World Register because it was the world's oldest existing movable metal type printed book. However, *Jikji* should exist not only for Korea but the entire world. Everyone in the world should know about this. Through such collective memory, people can build a global community and make commitments to sustainable development and peace. At the same time cultural heritages of the people in the past are passed down to future generations through people's collective memories and cultural memories. Humanity can leave cultural memories by maintaining cultural diversity and passing down cultural heritages created by human to future generations. *Jikji*, the Memory of the World, is a textbook to teach and learn Seon (禪, Zen) Buddhism. *Jikji* is the name of the book, but it is also a very important concept that symbolizes the spirit of cultivation. From this perspective, *Jikji* is a treasure for humanity that has spiritual value centered on education, experiment, and sincerity.

Currently, *Jikji* is housed in the National Library of France in Paris. This is why France, the owner, and Korea, the producer of *Jikji*, should cooperate with each other to capture its cultural and historical value. Korea also needs to respect the printing culture of other countries. In particular, it should respect France for its cultural discernment as it currently possesses and appreciates *Jikji*. At the same time, it should also acknowledge the value of the movable metal type of Gutenberg from Germany, which was used to print the 42-line Bibles and contributed to the mass production and distribution of information. These Bibles gave rise to the Renaissance, spread human-centered humanism, and contributed to the development of the capitalist. Movable metal type is important because of the significant meanings it carries and it is meaningful that Korea was the first nation that developed and used movable metal type. That is why countries that had advanced printing culture—such as Korea, Germany, France, Japan, China, and Switzerland—should respect and cooperate with each other.

References

Anderson, John Robert, Language, Memory, and Thought, (Hillsdale, New Jersy: Lawrence Erlbaum Associates, 1976).

Assmann, Jan, "Collective Memory and Cultural Identity", New German Critique, no 65, Cultural History/Cultural Studies, (Spring-Summer, 1995). pp.130-131.

Assmann, Jan, "Communicative and Cultural Memory", Cultural Memory Studies. An International and Interdisciplinary Handbook, (Berlin and New York, 2008), p.109.

Chungcheongbukdo Culture Charter, 2008.

Cheongju Citizen Charter.

Declaration of *Jikji* Globalization, Jun, 15, 2004.

Cheongju Chungcheongbukdo Korea "Early Printing Museum".

FINAL REPORT, Memory of the World Programme, UNESCO, Paris, August, 2001.

GENERAL GUIDELINES TO SAFEGUARD DOCUMENTARY HERITAGE. CII-95/WS-11rev February 2002

Halbwachs, Maurice, The collective memory, (New York: Harper & Row Colophon Books, 1980), p.31.

http://Jikjiworld.cheongju.go.kr/Jikjiworld/contents.do?key=17513 access Sep., 10, 2018.

http://unesdoc.unesco.org/images/0012/001256/125637e.pdf access Sep., 10, 2018.

Jeon, Gyeong-soo, "*Jikji* Translated by Cultural Theories" "The Modern Bibliography Review" 14, The Modern Bibliography Society, Dec. 2016.

Kim, Seung Hwan, "Creation of New Jikji Culture," Printing and Publishing Culture, Cheongju Early Printing Museum, 2000. p.124.

Kim, Seong-soo, "A Study on the Casting Pattern of Heungdeoksa Temple based on the Analytics of *Jikji*'s Printing State", 012 『Studies on Bibliography』56, The Institute of Korea Bibliography, Dec. 2013.

Kim, Hyeon-gi, "The Direction for Growth and Development of the Jikji Festival", "Journal of Korea Multimedia Society" 16(2), The Korea Multimedia Society, June 2012.

Lee, Sun-hee, "Collin de Plancy and *Jikji*: Focused on Korean Antique Books Housed in BULAC" "Journal of the Institute of Bibliography" 68, The Institute of Korea Bibliography, Dec. 2016.

Lee, Seung-cheol, "An Analytic Study on Movable Type pieces and Typesets Used to Print *Jikji*" "Journal of the Institute of Bibliography" 38, The Institute of Korea Bibliography, Dec. 2007.

Lee, Hee-jae, "*Baegun Hwasang Chorok Buljo Jikjisimcheyojeol* and Movable Type Printing Culture in Early Joseon" "Journal of the Institute of Bibliography" 28, The Institute of Korea Bibliography, Sep. 2004.

Nam, Yoon-seong, "The Meaning in Human History of Korea, the Inventor of Movable Metal Type and *Jikji*, the Memory of the World," "Journal of Korea Multimedia Society" 16(2), The Korea Multimedia Society, June 2012.

Park, Heu-sik, "The Meaning of *Jikji* in the History of Civilization and Visions for the *Jikji* Culture", "Journal of Hoseo Culture" 24, Seowon University *Jikji* Culture Industry Institute, Feb. 2015.

Hwang, Jeong-ha "Jikji, How It Was Published and Survived," "The Journal of History and Practical Thought Studies" 35, The Historical Society of Yeoksa Silhak, Jun. 2008.

UNESCO, Constitution. Article I Purposes and Functions.

UNESCO, UNIVERSAL DECLARATION ON CULTURAL DIVERSITY, 2001.

Generalization Oh, Youngtack
Planning Hwang Jeong-ha
Text Woo, Jinwoong / Choi, Kaungeun / Kim, Seunghwan
Edition Jang won-yeon
Translation Kim Juyeong
Supervision Tim Thompson

Date of publication 20th December 2018
Publisher Cheongju city / Cheongju Early Printing Museum

Cheongju Early Printing Museum
Address 713, Jikjidaero, Heungdeok-gu, Cheongju city,
Chungbuk Province, South Korea
Tel 043-201-4298 / Fax 043-201-4299
http://jikjiworld.cheongju.go.kr
Printer Ilgwang Co., Ltd
12, 204Bungil, Sangdangro, Sangdang-gu, Cheongju city,
Chungbuk Province, South Korea
Tel 043-221-2948

Registration number of publication 73-5710016-000011-14

ISBN 978-89-6771-128-3
ISBN 978-89-6771-128-3 (전3권)

緣化
門人

施主比丘尼

釋璨
遠湛
妙德

名為智於入佛不思議

承古種師常勸諸人莫學佛法但向無心去利根

人盡時解脫鈍根人或三五年遂不過十年若不

悟去老僧替你入拔舌

白雲和尚抄錄佛祖直指心體要節卷下

宣光七年丁巳七月　日　清州牧外興德

寺鑄字印施